Crime Prevention and Security Management

Series Editor
Martin Gill, Perpetuity Research, Tunbridge Wells, UK

It is widely recognized that we live in an increasingly unsafe society, but the study of security and crime prevention has lagged behind in its importance on the political agenda and has not matched the level of public concern. This exciting new series aims to address these issues looking at topics such as crime control, policing, security, theft, workplace violence and crime, fear of crime, civil disorder, white collar crime and anti-social behaviour. International in perspective, providing critically and theoretically-informed work, and edited by a leading scholar in the field, this series will advance new understandings of crime prevention and security management.

Tim Prenzler

Preventing Crime and Disorder in Public Places

Blending Opportunity Reduction, Guardianship and Welfare

Tim Prenzler
School of Law and Society
University of the Sunshine Coast
Sippy Downs, QLD, Australia

ISSN 2946-3513   ISSN 2946-3521   (electronic)
Crime Prevention and Security Management
ISBN 978-3-031-63763-6   ISBN 978-3-031-63764-3   (eBook)
https://doi.org/10.1007/978-3-031-63764-3

Cover illustration: © Melisa Hasan

This Palgrave Macmillan imprint is published by the registered company Springer Nature Switzerland AG
The registered company address is: Gewerbestrasse 11, 6330 Cham, Switzerland

If disposing of this product, please recycle the paper.

Series Editor's Introduction

Linking theory to practice in security research is very much underdeveloped; most studies focus on either theory or practice and at best refer to the other and mostly fleetingly. What marks out this book, as the author Tim Prenzler notes, is that it is presented as "a readily accessible guide that combines theoretical insights with 'do-able' strategies that can be applied by responsible parties on their home turf."

Chapter 1 both describes and explains the causes of the range of crimes committed in public places and applies the crime triangle to guide prevention. Chapter 2 looks at the principles behind designing out crime and how they can be used to develop crime prevention approaches. The book then devotes chapters to different topics and problems that crime and disorder pose. Chapter 3 focusses on security patrols partnering with police and other agencies to extend the broader policing service to the public. Chapter 4 assesses how improvements in local amenities can help tackle social exclusion.

Chapter 5 focusses on road safety where issues such as fare evasion and graffiti are also tackled. Chapter 6 discusses approaches to managing locales where alcohol is served to increase users' enjoyment while at the same time managing the risk of conflict. Chapter 7 looks at public gatherings—from entertainment to protests—and we learn how these can be best managed. Chapter 8, unusually, discusses public toilets and how they can be used to make spaces attractive to legitimate users. The final chapter brings all these discussions together with a discussion of a four-step model to guide the design and implementation of intervention programs.

The chapters in this book are easy to follow and all provide an evidence base for policy. The Pivot Series was designed for just this purpose and this is an excellent example that I am delighted we can bring to you.

April 2024   Martin Gill

Preface

Despite the growth of the internet and online 'spaces', humans remain a physically interactive and networked species. We constantly engage with each other face-to-face, or in close proximity, in situations that facilitate friendship, entertainment, government, commerce and crime. Sadly, conflict and crime are often concentrated in places where people congregate, and the confluence of potential offenders and victims requires specialist management strategies to ensure safety and tranquillity. With this goal in mind, the book provides scientifically informed guidance on effective place management strategies. It integrates theoretical perspectives and practical examples of crime prevention and disorder abatement methods which can be readily implemented by responsible authorities and stakeholder groups. Applicable locations include town centres, shopping malls, parks, beaches, transit hubs, campuses, stadiums and entertainment precincts. These are places where security programs sometimes attract criticisms regarding the exclusion or persecution of marginalised groups. How to address the needs and rights of these groups is a major co-concern of the book.

Many books on crime prevention are large, complex and highly academic. The market is missing a readily accessible guide that combines theoretical insights with 'do-able' strategies that can be applied by responsible parties on their home turf. With this in mind, in keeping with the spirit of the Palgrave Pivot series, the book is in a short format—just long enough to get the core ideas and evidence across from a complex field without becoming overly-detailed and tedious. The nine chapters are all concise, punchy and easy-to-read. I am particularly hopeful that the book will appeal to a variety of busy professionals engaged in designing or doing crime prevention and working in the welfare sector. These include government policy officers; frontline police and police managers; security officers and security managers; crime prevention specialists; politicians; town planners; crime prevention and CPTED trainers; and social workers and youth outreach workers. The book is also suitable as source material for teachers and researchers in academic settings.

My teaching and research in crime prevention over 30 years has been focused on documented case studies as a way to understand what can work in stopping crime. Theory is important for identifying causes of crime and disorder and likely successful preventive measures, but case studies provide the tests that are needed to verify the theory. In keeping with this approach, readers will be introduced to a wide range of successful programs as well as the central role of a generic problem-solving methodology. *Preventing Crime and Disorder in Public Places* is distinctive in its focus on real-life cases. The book is also distinctive in advocating overlapping forms of crime prevention and social support which address the need to make large improvements in public safety while supporting marginalised and vulnerable groups. It brings together the disciplines of applied crime prevention, policing, security management, social work and town planning.

The development of this book overlapped with an applied project on crime prevention conducted with my local authority, the Sunshine Coast Council. The work was conducted with colleagues Emily Moir and Sue Rayment-McHugh. Some of the material included in the book was found by our excellent Research Associate Nat Cairns. Nat's ideas and judgements were also of great value, as were Emily's and Sue's. The two large reports from this project are available via the following links: https://research.usc.edu.au/esploro/outputs/report/Nambour-Community-Safety-Review-Stage-1/99680498102621?institution=61USC_INST, https://research.usc.edu.au/esploro/outputs/report/Nambour-Community-Safety-Review-Phase-2/99745898502621?institution=61USC_INST.

Chapter 1 of the book—Diagnosing Crime and Disorder Problems in Public Places—begins by describing the numerous and diverse crime-related problems that occur in public places—especially 'street crimes'—and the main causes. Attention is initially given to major social structural influences, including poverty, inequality, social disorganisation and government neglect. The focus then shifts to areas of opportunity where local authorities can make a difference. The crime triangle—outlining the intersection of 'offender, target/victim and place'—is posited as an essential starting point for in-depth examinations of situational factors facilitating locally based crime and disorder problems with a view to designing interventions with the best chance of success.

Chapter 2—Creating Defensible Spaces and Designing Out Opportunities for Crime—focuses on situational prevention and CPTED (Crime Prevention Through Environmental Design) as the best guides for operationalising effective preventive strategies including facilitating compliance and enlarging guardianship—with numerous practical examples. Additional applied theories include community policing, reassurance policing, quality-of-life policing and third-party policing. Social contract theory and systematic problem solving (or 'problem-oriented policing') constitute the overarching frameworks for success.

Chapters 3 to 8 then develop these approaches in depth in relation to a set of specific topic areas and types of crime and disorder problems. Chapter 3—Combining Police and Security Patrols with Welfare Services—examines the evidence in support of visible uniformed foot patrols by traditional law enforcement officers—public and/or private—with the addition of a large welfare component to their work. This can be extended through partnerships with welfare specialists, such as mental health crisis intervention professionals and social workers engaged in services to persons affected by drug dependence or homelessness. This theme is continued in Chapter 4—Business Improvement, Urban Regeneration and Social Inclusion—which examines how programs to improve the amenity and safety of an area—in order to improve commerce and the public enjoyment of open spaces—can work with on-site services for disadvantaged persons.

The next chapter is concerned with the topic of Safe Orderly and Efficient Transport Systems. This includes consideration of a wide range of strategies to improve road safety and mitigate the adverse effects of motor vehicles on the urban environment. Other issues addressed include graffiti, vandalism, fare evasion, assaults, commuter insecurity and network inefficiencies. Chapter 6—Reducing Intoxication and Alcohol-related Crime in Entertainment Precincts—examines ways to optimise people's enjoyment of pubs, clubs and other entertainment venues without conflict and violence. The following chapter titled Safe Events: Festivals, Sports and Protests—continues the theme of managing large gatherings to ensure purposes, such as entertainment, are balanced with safety and security. The chapter includes a case study of democratic management of the right to peaceful protest.

Chapter 8 is titled Public Toilets Matter! It shows how easy it is for public authorities—genuinely committed to the wellbeing of their constituents and visitors—to provide for one of the most basic needs of human nature in a way that is private, clean, comfortable and safe while also attracting legitimate users to a public area.

The final chapter—It's a Process: Best Practice in Preventing Crime and Disorder in Public Places—goes behind the case studies in the book to identify the most efficient, effective and fair means of managing crime prevention programs. A four-step model and checklist covers all the main issues in program design and implementation to ensure the best chances of success.

In conclusion, I would like to thank the team at Palgrave Macmillan who encouraged and supported the development of this book: Josie Taylor, Martin Gill and Shreenidhi Natarajan. I would also like to thank the anonymous reviewer for their positive response to the proposal and helpful advice.

Sippy Downs, QLD, Australia   Tim Prenzler

CONTENTS

About the Author

Tim Prenzler is a Professor of Criminology in the School of Law and Society at the University of the Sunshine Coast (UniSC) Australia. He was the foundation Coordinator of the Bachelor of Criminology and Justice from 2015 to 2018. He has developed and taught courses in introductory criminology, policing, crime prevention, and ethics and integrity management in criminal justice. He has been a recipient of UniSC's Vice-Chancellor's Award for Excellence in Learning and Teaching and the Australian and New Zealand Society of Criminology's (ANZSOC) Excellence and Innovation in Teaching Award.

Tim's research interests include crime and corruption prevention, police and security officer safety, security industry regulation, gender equity in policing and restorative justice. He has engaged in numerous pro bono and funded research projects with private security and criminal justice agencies. He has been a recipient of the ANZSOC Adam Sutton Crime Prevention Research Award on two occasions and the ANZSOC David Biles Correctional Research Award.

Tim's books include *Police Early Intervention Systems: Integrating Officer Performance, Integrity and Welfare* (2024, Springer, with Louise Porter), *Gender Inclusive Policing* (2023, Routledge), *Ethics and Accountability in Criminal Justice* (2021, Australian Academic Press), *Regulating the Security Industry: Global Perspectives* (2018, Routledge, with Mahesh Nalla), *Understanding Crime Prevention: The Case Study Approach* (2017, Australian Academic Press), *Civilian Oversight of Police:*

Advancing Accountability in Law Enforcement (2016, Taylor & Francis, with Garth den Heyer), *Policing and Security in Practice: Challenges and Achievements* (2016, Palgrave Macmillan), *One Hundred Years of Women Police in Australia* (2015, Australian Academic Press), *Contemporary Police Practice* (2015, Oxford University Press, with Jaqueline Drew), *Understanding and Preventing Corruption* (2013, Palgrave, with Adam Graycar), *The Law of Private Security in Australia* (2009, Thomson, with Rick Sarre) and *Police Corruption: Preventing Misconduct and Maintaining Integrity* (2009, Taylor & Francis).

LIST OF FIGURES

LIST OF TABLES

CHAPTER 1

Diagnosing Crime and Disorder Problems in Public Places

Abstract This introductory chapter maps out the main types of crime-related problems occurring in public places, covering a wide spectrum from bag snatching to harassment to drug dealing to mass shootings. Physical disorder is also given attention. Background factors include inequality, social disorganisation and government and management neglect. An opportunity perspective sets out the immediate influences acting on these problems. For example, routine activity theory and the crime triangle highlight how public places provide fertile hunting grounds for offenders, with large numbers of vulnerable victims and inadequate guardianship. Overall, the chapter shows that crime and disorder in public places are major social problems with serious adverse effects on people's lives. Authorities need to be more responsive and step up to do all that can be done legally and ethically to create safe harmonious public spaces.

Keywords Street offences · Hot spots · Opportunity theories · Risky settings

© The Author(s), under exclusive license to Springer Nature
Switzerland AG 2024
T. Prenzler, *Preventing Crime and Disorder in Public Places*, Crime
Prevention and Security Management,
https://doi.org/10.1007/978-3-031-63764-3_1

TYPES OF OFFENCES

This book is concerned with crime, disorder and associated problems, such as urban blight, occurring in settings that can loosely be termed 'public places'. These are locations where people often congregate in large numbers. Many of these places are government-controlled and open access—such as town centres, open street malls, parks and entertainment precincts—where it is difficult to exclude people intent on committing crimes. Other locations, often also involving government property, involve capacity for restrictions, such as transport systems. In such cases, access to the foyer area might be open while access to train carriages or buses is controlled by ticketing. 'Mass private property' (Shearing & Stenning, 1981, p. 228) or 'privately owned public spaces' (Kayden, 2000) involve private property that is often open access for large numbers of persons. Examples include enclosed shopping malls, sporting arenas and concert venues. Although it is possible to place restrictions on likely offenders—based on offence histories, for example—this can be hard to do in practice. Excluding people is often against access policies that encourage attendance by large numbers of potential customers or participants.

Public places—whether publicly or privately owned—are subject to a large variety of criminal attacks, both on people and property. Many of these forms of abuse come under the unofficial title of 'street crime'. This is a useful, if inexact, term. Mazerolle (2015, p. 119), provides the following description:

> Street crimes include not-so-serious incidents that occur 'on the streets,' in public parks, at railway stations, and low-level incidents that occur inside venues like clubs and pubs. Street crimes include drug dealing, prostitution, street assaults, street robberies, graffiti, vandalism, social incivilities and social and physical disorder. These are the types of crimes that generally involve exchange of small quantities of drugs, prostitutes soliciting from the street (as opposed to prostitution via an escort agency or brothel), handbag snatches and robberies, graffiti and vandalism on train stations, brawls in clubs, pubs and public places. Street crimes are the types of incidents that occur mainly in the evening hours and on weekend nights. Fights break out late on a Saturday night outside a bar. Broken glass is scattered about in a city mall. Bus stops are vandalised. Prostitutes solicit clients from a street corner. Small quantities of illicit pills are sold inside nightclubs. A purse is stolen from a restaurant. A car window in a parking

lot is smashed and CDs are stolen. These are all examples of relatively minor street crimes that consume large amounts of police time.

These street offences include 'disorderly conduct' and overlap with the large problem of 'disorder' in public places. According to Mazerolle (2015, p. 121),

> Disorder offences include low-level incidents like people urinating in public, yelling on the streets, throwing and smashing empty bottles, leaving condoms and drug paraphernalia lying around, breaking seats in a mall, harassing people as they walk by, being drunk in public, and blocking footpaths and streets. Disorder problems are sometimes referred to as 'incivilities' and often split into social (e.g. lewd acts, loitering) and physical (e.g. broken windows, broken bottles) categories.

These definitions and examples point to a very wide range of anti-social behaviours, and we could add many other examples including smoking and speeding scooters. Although described as 'not-so-serious', this is a relative term, comparing these offences to major crimes like murder, armed robbery, mass shootings and bombings. Most victims of street crimes will feel they have suffered significant personal harm, and the proliferation of these behaviours has a cumulative effect that can drive people away from an area or impair their ability to enjoy being out and about. And, of course, crimes occurring in public places are not limited to this category. Murder, more serious assaults, sexual assaults and armed robberies often occur in public places or overlap with public places. A fight in a nightclub can spillover onto the footpath. A motor vehicle theft from a residence can develop into a dangerous police vehicle pursuit.

Also of importance here is the idea of physical disorder. People can feel affronted and unsafe in an environment that is unsightly and characterised by disrepair and decay. To the list above, we can add problems like potholes, broken concrete, weeds, empty shops, boarded-up premises, poor lighting, overgrown gardens, barking dogs, dog fouling, loud music, hooning, traffic congestion, parking congestion and parking violations.

Historically, modern public sector policing was developed to address an upsurge of street crime in the late 1700s and early 1800s in the British Isles, and the commonality of these problems in town and city centres drove the adoption of the uniformed beat policing model around the world from that time (Drew & Prenzler, 2015, chapter 1). Street crimes and other crimes occurring in public places continue to take up a great deal of police resources and challenge police tactics (Berkley & Thayer, 2000). People look to the police for protection, but experiences of crime and feelings of insecurity in these places also drive dissatisfaction with the police (see Chapter 3, Combining Police and Security Patrols with Welfare Services).

DIAGNOSES

The remainder of this chapter deals with the causal factors behind these problems. The primary purpose of understanding causes should be to guide effective crime prevention strategies. With that large goal in mind, diagnosing problems of crime and disorder in public places is not particularly difficult. In fact, many factors that people are likely to intuit, such as inequality, lack of guardianship and under-policing, are supported by research and are often easily translated into successful preventive interventions—as we will see in further chapters of this book.

SOCIAL STRUCTURAL CONTEXTS

Readers with a background in criminology will be aware that there is an array of named theories of crime. While many of them appear mutually exclusive, they often also have some value in explaining aspects of crime. Theories can be categorised into three main types—psychological, sociological and situational. Situational—or opportunity factors—constitute the focus of the next section of this chapter and of the whole book. Nonetheless, it should be kept in mind that psychological and sociological—or social structural—factors have relevance to the contexts of crime in public places. There are useful integrated frameworks that bring these together. For example, Durrant and Ward (2015) discuss three main macro-level factors that predispose people to crime: 'individual' (based on personality factors like impulsivity and poor self-control), 'family' (especially neglect, conflict and erratic discipline) and 'social' (including relative inequality, deprived neighbourhoods and delinquent peers) (p. 158). Some people predisposed to crime will be attracted to public places in search of vulnerable victims. In other cases, less driven people might fall into crime when they see an opportunity or are provoked in a public setting.

Social Disorganisation

When it comes to high-crime locations, the sociological theory of 'social disorganisation' is of particular value in understanding the high rates of crime often apparent in inner-city locations (Bull, 2020). These areas, generally located between safer central business districts and middle-class suburbs, are often characterised by multiple social pathologies. Higher crime rates are accompanied by a greater fear of crime as well as high rates of suicide, mental illness, poverty, unemployment and urban decay. One explanation for this situation, based on social ecology theory, is that these areas are characterised by 'anomie' or high rates of 'social disorganisation'. Normal social bonds through family, peers and community leaders are broken down by poverty, unemployment and transitory lifestyles. Impoverished and alienated persons are forced into cheap squalid rentals and anonymity drives stranger crimes. This situation can be triggered by diverse factors including rapid immigration, war, colonisation and economic collapse and can also affect rural communities, towns and suburbs.

Broken Windows

Mention should also be made here of broken windows theory, which developed out of social ecology theory and the concept of social disorganisation. In the article 'Broken windows: The police and neighbourhood safety', Wilson and Kelling (1982) developed the image of unrepaired broken windows as a metaphor for how communities can deteriorate and shift from attractive safe places where neighbours provide collective security to crime-ridden unattractive ghettos where people are afraid to go outside. This snowball process is described in the following scenario (p. 31):

> A piece of property is abandoned, weeds grow up, a window is smashed. Adults stop scolding rowdy children; the children, emboldened, become more rowdy. Families move out, unattached adults move in. Teenagers gather in front of the corner store. The merchant asks them to move; they refuse. Fights occur. Litter accumulates. People start drinking in front of the grocery; in time, an inebriate slumps to the sidewalk and is allowed to sleep it off. Pedestrians are approached by panhandlers.
>
> At this point it is not inevitable that serious crime will flourish or violent attacks on strangers will occur. But many residents will think that

crime, especially violent crime, is on the rise, and they will modify their behaviour accordingly. They will use the streets less often, and when on the streets will stay apart from their fellows, moving with averted eyes, silent lips, and hurried steps. 'Don't get involved.' For some residents, this growing atomization will matter little, because the neighbourhood is not their 'home' but 'the place where they live.' Their interests are elsewhere; they are cosmopolitans. But it will matter greatly to other people, whose lives derive meaning and satisfaction from local attachments rather than worldly involvement; for them, the neighbourhood will cease to exist except for a few reliable friends whom they arrange to meet.

Such an area is vulnerable to criminal invasion. Though it is not inevitable, it is more likely that here, rather than in places where people are confident they can regulate public behaviour by informal controls, drugs will change hands, prostitutes will solicit, and cars will be stripped.

Broken windows theory includes the idea that signs of disorder encourage disorderly conduct and that this has a contagion effect. There is some evidence to support this idea. For example, Keiser et al. (2008) conducted a set of field experiments in which subjects in disorderly environments (with graffiti and litter, for example) were more likely to litter, trespass and steal than those in orderly environments—supporting the view that people tend to conform to the behavioural norms apparent around them (see also Gabor, 1994). The shift in policing to motorised patrols, away from foot patrols and personalised order maintenance work, is also a causal factor in urban decay according to Wilson and Kelling. An additional related concept is 'collective efficacy', which captures the idea of community members working together to protect each other—something that is usually lost under anomic conditions (Sampson et al., 1997).

Another key concept here is that of visual disorder and its effects on potential offenders and guardians. According to the broken windows thesis, signs of physical neglect—such as graffiti and disrepair—signal a lack of guardianship that attracts offenders. At the same time, potential guardians are deterred because of fear of victimisation. Reversing this self-reinforcing cycle is a key requirement for creating safe and orderly public places. It should be kept in mind that these areas are often attractive to artists and non-conformists, and this subculture can also provide a basis for urban regeneration in part by attracting musicians, artists and boutique stores.

Government Policies, Under-resourcing and Under-regulation

Under-resourcing is a major explanation for inadequate public security (e.g., Barclay et al., 1997, p. 147). Part of this is a 'structural' explanation related to the lack of resources and authority held by local governments. In many locations, policing and crime prevention are largely local government responsibilities. The United States is a prime example. However, local governments are often restricted to 'regressive' taxation as a source of funds, that is taxes, such as property taxes, that apply to persons regardless of their income (Varela, 2015). Local governments are reluctant to raise these taxes to adequately resource social services, such as beat police or homeless shelters, because of the negative effect the taxes have on middle- and lower-income residents. 'Progressive' taxation—primarily income tax that increases as incomes increase—is often controlled by higher levels of government with no or limited responsibility for localised crime problems.

The author's home country, Australia, is a prime example of this problem, referred to as a 'vertical fiscal imbalance' (Galligan, 2014). The bulk of taxes are collected by the federal government, including company and personal income taxes, but the states are responsible for most social services—including policing, health and housing. Local governments were historically concerned with 'roads, rates and rubbish' (Chou et al., 2023). However, increasing community concerns over crime have forced councils to take on responsibilities for public safety (Prenzler & Wilson, 2019). For example, the construction of open-air malls in town centres, by closing off streets, often led to problems of concentrated disorder that resulted in councils having to act on crime mitigation. It is not uncommon for state police and local leaders to be at odds over priorities for crime control in local settings. In some cases, councils took on security programs—primarily involving camera systems and security guards—which were outside their normal budget parameters.

The under-resourcing of public protection can be sheeted home to a complex set of fiscal problems that beset most countries. Chief amongst them is the failure to tax the rich, especially the super-rich who accrue personal wealth far beyond anything they can possibly spend (Neate, 2020). These individuals, and numerous transnational companies, benefit from the legal settings and social conditions established by governments and communities where they operate, but they do not pay back a fair share of their profits. Part of the explanation for this is their ability to exploit tax loopholes and park their money in places out of the reach of tax authorities. One estimate put global losses to tax havens in 2023 at US$48 billion (Tax Justice Network, 2023, p. 13). The failure of democratic governments to shut down money laundering schemes is an overlapping problem.

Wasteful government expenditure involves another major misdirection of public funds (Prenzler, 2021), some of which should be invested in public space security programs. Subsidisation of fossil fuel use in the face of the climate change crisis is one example. The International Monetary Fund (2023) reported that in 2022 governments spent US$7 trillion supporting fossil fuel industries. Corruption is another major source of lost resources for public safety. The United Nations estimates that corruption—in terms of bribes paid and money stolen—involves an average of US$3 trillion in lost public sector spending each year (United Nations, 2023).

Under-resourcing: Homelessness

Homelessness represents a problem of disorder common in many city centres (D'Souza, 2020). Causal factors include poverty, unemployment, drug addiction, mental illness and family conflict. People in these situations are often attracted to public places where they feel safer, where they can beg for money and where they can access services such as soup kitchens. Apart from the discomfort, ill-health and insecurity experienced by homeless persons, this phenomenon can create general problems of hygiene, aggressive begging, fear of crime and commercial decline. Local authorities can provide accommodation, employment and health services on-site. However, these are often expensive and compete in the budget against traditional local government expenditures. Services can also attract more clients, and vocal business owners and shoppers often prefer that homeless people are moved on (Prenzler et al., 2022, chapter 4).

The United States has one of the most visible forms of public homelessness. Loitering, people sleeping rough and homeless camps blight many city centres, and the problem is largely the result of a substandard health and welfare system, involving inadequate redistributive taxation at the national level (Shinn, 2010). This issue, and the more general problem of substandard public services, is captured well by the famous reference to 'private affluence and public squalor' in the United States by economist John Galbraith (Pedestrian Observations, 2019). It is true that many welfare states struggle with homelessness, but a generous welfare system, including a large public housing program, provides the context for localised support services. From a social contract perspective (Chapter 2), laws against vagrancy, begging or loitering need to be offset by the availability of accommodation, employment and income support.

Under-regulation: Mass Shootings and Gun Crime

Mass shootings provide an example of a devastating crime that frequently occurs in public spaces but about which local authorities appear helpless. Mass shootings can be largely eliminated by a strict gun licensing and registration system that bans automatic weapons and includes eligibility, training and storage requirements and an inspection regime (Lemieux et al., 2022). This standard system can also substantially reduce other gun crimes, like murder and armed robbery, as well as suicides and gun-related accidents. The legislation needs to be enacted at the national level because of free movement across local and state boundaries. The refusal of governments to introduce strict gun controls, despite large majority support from the public, means that local authorities are left to deal with the aftermath—in part through attempted containment procedures occurring once a shooting event has begun.

OPPORTUNITY THEORIES

The perspectives set out briefly above provide useful background explanations for crime. However, the practical implications for prevention are often not developed by national and state/provincial governments, and local authorities, business owners and community groups are limited in their capacity to address long-term psychological and large-scale social structural causes of crime. In such cases, situationally-focused opportunity theories provide the best guidance for designing interventions with immediate effects. Despite limitations and exceptions—such as mass shootings (above)—there is often a lot that place managers can do to change the environmental factors that facilitate crime (while also lobbying governments for better macro-level prevention programs).

Routine activity theory is an example of an opportunity theory that provides useful concepts for understanding the potential for crime in areas where people congregate. In that regard, Cohen and Felson (1979) outline the minimal requirements for crime to occur through 'the convergence in space and time of ... (1) motivated offenders, (2) suitable targets, and (3) the absence of capable guardians' (p. 589). This approach overlaps with contributions from rational choice theory, which analyses how potential offenders make decisions based on the perceived costs and benefits of committing crime in the context of situational factors that maximise or minimise the risks and rewards (Cornish & Clarke, 1986). These approaches take for granted the fact that many people will come to public places predisposed to commit crimes or are triggered to commit crimes when they perceive an opportunity. Offenders will commit crimes because they think they can, that is because they calculate they will obtain a benefit from an illicit act and get away with it.

The Crime Triangle

The crime triangle—Fig. 1.1—is a model that usefully captures the core elements of victim–offender encounters and adds countervailing elements to reduce opportunities (Clarke & Eck, 2003). The inner triangle summarises the three primary ingredients for crime: an offender, a target and a place. This overlaps with Cohen and Felson's concept (above) of an offender and a target who converge in space and time in the absence of an effective guardian. The following chapter—Creating Defensible Spaces and Designing Out Opportunities for Crime—looks at interventions at each of these points at the outer triangle.

As an explanation for crime, the inner triangle might seem to be an example of the 'blindingly obvious'. However, the implications are frequently ignored, especially in terms of designing preventive interventions based on closing off opportunities. For example, town centres and entertainment areas obviously attract people involved in shopping, carrying out business and seeking entertainment and recreation. The combination of large numbers of diverse goods and services for sale, and different types of people, creates numerous opportunities for crime by attracting potential offenders and bringing them into contact with potential victims. These victims are often busy and distracted and carrying crime targets of value, such as wallets, bags and mobile phones. The disinhibiting effects of alcohol often escalate these risks. In an unregulated environment, these conditions will facilitate crime. Crime prevention analytics will, however, examine what changes can be made with the offender, the target/victim and/or the place to reduce the chances of

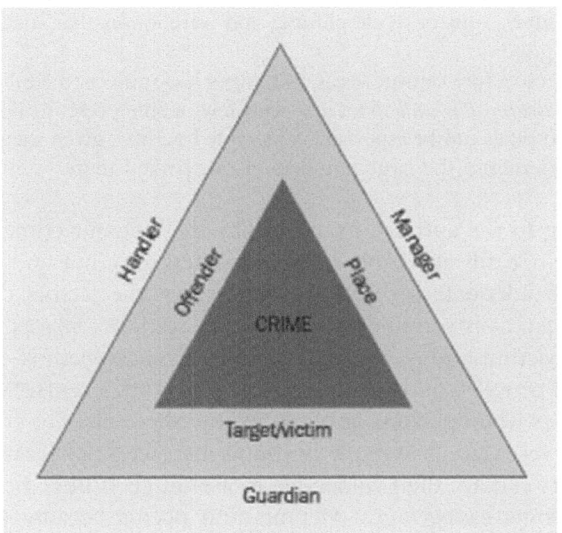

Fig. 1.1 The crime triangle (*Source* Clarke & Eck, 2003, p. 9. Used with permission)

victimisation occurring. The crime triangle therefore provides the basis for more complex crime pattern analyses, usually computer-based, to specify types of offences, when and where they are concentrated, and profiles of offenders and victims, in order to generate a tailor-made site-specific explanatory picture of localised crime problems.

Risky Settings, Risky Facilities and Hot Spots for Crime

The concept of risky places is also of value in understanding concentrations of crime and disorderly conduct. Felson and Eckert's (2019) list of common 'risky settings' for crime includes locations that are all essentially 'public spaces' (p. 26):

Public routes, especially foot paths, parking facilities, and unsupervised transit areas; this includes public transit settings, stations, and bus stops
Recreation settings, including barrooms as well as informal hangouts where teenagers avoid parental controls

Retail stores, subject to shoplifting, and warehouses that store valuable electronic goods

Schools, especially outside areas and edges less subject to adult control

Large parking lots and structures with few people present for security.

Even hospitals can be especially vulnerable to crime, given their 24-hour activity pattern and the large numbers of cars parked there.

According to the authors, locations like these favour crime because of the presence of easily accessible attractive targets for crime and the absence of natural or adequate protections. Analysis of the factors that make a 'suitable target' assists in understanding risky settings—places that experience repeat victimisation—and their corollary, repeat victims—individuals or groups of people who experience successive crime events. 'Victim facilitation' occurs when persons or places expose themselves to crime. At the individual level, a good example is young men who deliberately become drunk in bars and are then vulnerable to assault (Felson & Eckert, 2019, p. 35). In some cases, repeat victimisation occurs because a successful crime will motivate offenders to return to the same location, often within a short time frame, such as a month (Bowers et al., 1998).

Eck et al. (2007) focused on the concept of negligent 'place management' as a major explanation for 'risky facilities'. Place managers can be responsible, often unconsciously, for management practices that are 'crime enablers':

The concentration of crime at a few facilities can seldom be dismissed as a random fluke or 'just a lot of targets' or active offenders... Comparing the way similar facilities with different crime levels are managed can test crime enabling. If compared to low crime facilities, the high crime locations have fewer rules, lax enforcement, easy access, poor security, and other features that help offenders detect targets, commit crimes, and get away... If the high crime facilities have many targets or more highly desirable targets (either hot products or repeat victims) compared to low crime facilities, but managers do little to enhance target protection, this also suggests place management is at the heart of the problem. (2007, p. 240)

An example is that of pubs and clubs that inadvertently encourage violence through alcohol sales gimmicks which increase consumption and intoxication. They also fail to provide services, such as food and entertainment, which can reduce intoxication (Felson & Eckert, 2019,

p. 29; see Chapter 6, Reducing Intoxication and Alcohol-related Crime in Entertainment Precincts).

Risky places are where crime is concentrated, and these locations are also referred to as crime 'hot spots'—a term which can encompass larger geographical zones such as street corners and intersections, parks and squares. In their work on this topic, Sherman et al. (1989) analysed police data in the city of Minneapolis and found calls for police assistance were far from evenly distributed. Across one year (p. 37),

> Just over half (50.4%) of all calls to the police for which cars were dispatched went to a mere 3.3% of all addresses and intersections... The number of calls per location ranged as high as 810 at a large discount store near a poor neighborhood, followed by 686 calls at a large department store, 607 calls at a corner with a 24-hours-a-day convenience store and a bar, and 479 calls at a public housing apartment building.

The researchers observed that many of these locations were probably safe for most members of the public. Many of the calls involved shoplifters, for example, or noise complaints. However more dangerous 'predatory crimes ... generally committed in public places' were more highly concentrated. Specifically, 'all 4,166 robbery calls were located at only 2.2% ... of all places, all 3,908 auto thefts at 2.7% ..., and all 1,729 rape/CSCs (criminal sexual conduct) at just 1.2% ... of the places in the city' (p. 39).

This type of analysis represents a first step in addressing crime problems in public spaces. What is needed as a next step, according to the authors, are analyses that identify environmental factors that attract crime to these locations. Hot spots demonstrate consistently high rates of crime, with some fluctuations, often applying over many years. Consequently, another valid follow-up question concerns why relevant authorities have allowed these problems to persist. The factors that cause this phenomenon might be situational—i.e., the mingling of attractive victims and competent offenders—in what might be considered natural settings—such as entertainment areas where people are less inhibited. At the same time, it is the responsibility of authorities to intervene to prevent victimisation.

CONCLUSION

Crime and disorder in public places involve a disturbing variety of forms, entailing a formidable challenge for place managers. Neglect by authorities, the failure to fund protection services and the failure to tax appropriately are background factors that need to be addressed at the contextual level. At the more nuanced local level, public places include hotspots where crime is highly concentrated. These locations contain an array of goods that attract property crime offenders. Large numbers of distracted shoppers and visitors also become targets for violent offences. Public places frequently involve easy access and exit routes. These factors create volatile intersections for driven and opportunistic offenders and attractive vulnerable targets—with absent or inadequate guardians. The concept of risky places is important in understanding negligent management practices that exacerbate aspects of these natural settings for crime. The next chapter shows how these aspects of crime causation can be turned around to make public places safe, enjoyable and vibrant.

REFERENCES

Barclay, P., Buckley, J., Brantingham, P., Brantingham, P., & Whin-Yates, T. (1997). Preventing auto theft in commuter lots: A bike patrol in Vancouver. In R. Clarke (Ed.), *Situational crime prevention: Successful case studies* (pp. 143–156). Harrow and Heston.

Berkley, J., & Thayer, R. (2000). Policing entertainment districts. *Policing: An International Journal of Police Strategies and Management, 23*(4), 466–491.

Bowers, K., Hirschfield, A., & Johnson, S. (1998). Victimization revisited: A case study of non-residential repeat burglary on Merseyside. *British Journal of Criminology, 38*(3), 429–452.

Bull, M. (2020). Social explanations. In H. Hayes & T. Prenzler (Eds.), *An Introduction to crime and criminology* (pp. 210–227). Pearson.

Chou, M., Busbridge, R., & Rutledge-Prior, S. (2023, February 16). Beyond roads, rates and rubbish: Australians now expect local councils to act on bigger issues, including climate change. *The Conversation.* https://theconver sation.com/beyond-roads-rates-and-rubbish-australians-now-expect-local-cou ncils-to-act-on-bigger-issues-including-climate-change-199861

Clarke, R., & Eck, J. (2003). *Become a problem solving crime analysis in 55 small steps.* https://popcenter.asu.edu/sites/default/files/55stepsuk_0_0.pdf

Cohen, L., & Felson, M. (1979). Social change and crime rate trends: A routine activity approach. *American Sociological Review, 44*(August), 588–608.

Cornish, D., & Clarke, R. (Eds.). (1986). *The reasoning criminal*. Springer-Verlag.

D'Souza, A. (2020). An examination of order maintenance policing by business improvement districts. *Journal of Contemporary Criminal Justice, 36*(1), 70–85.

Drew, J., & Prenzler, T. (2015). *Contemporary police practice*. Oxford University Press.

Durrant, R., & Ward, T. (2015). *Evolutionary criminology: Towards a comprehensive explanation of crime*. Elsevier.

Eck, J., Clarke, R., & Guerette, R. (2007). Risky Facilities. *Crime Prevention Studies, 21*, 225–264.

Felson, M., & Eckert, M. (2019). *Crime and everyday life: A brief introduction*. SAGE.

Gabor, T. (1994). *Everybody does it! Crime by the public*. University of Toronto Press.

Galligan, B. (2014, September 15). Renewing federalism: What are the solutions to vertical fiscal imbalance? *The Conversation*. https://theconversation.com/renewing-federalism-what-are-the-solutions-to-vertical-fiscal-imbalance-31422

International Monetary Fund. (2023). *Fossil fuel subsidies*. https://www.imf.org/en/Topics/climate-change/energy-subsidies#:~:text=Back%20to%20Top-,Size%20of%20Fossil%20Fuel%20Subsidies,support%20from%20surging%20energy%20prices

Kayden, J. (2000). *Privately owned public space: The New York City experience*. Wiley.

Keiser, K., Lindenberg, S., & Steg, L. (2008, November 20). The spreading of disorder. *Science Express* (pp. 1–6).

Lemieux, F., Prenzler, T., & Bricknell, S. (2022). Mass shootings and gun control by police: Comparing Australia and the United States. In W. Wallace (Ed.), *Guns, gun violence and gun homicides: Perspectives from the global south* (pp. 29–52). Palgrave Macmillan.

Mazerolle, L. (2015). Street crime. In H. Hayes & T. Prenzler (Eds.), *An introduction to crime and criminology* (pp. 118–133). Pearson.

Neate, R. (2020, July 13). *Super-rich call for higher taxes on wealthy to pay for Covid-19 recovery*. https://www.theguardian.com/news/2020/jul/13/super-rich-call-for-higher-taxes-on-wealthy-to-pay-for-covid-19-recovery

Pedestrian Observations. (2019, November 18). *What Does Private Affluence, Public Squalor Mean?* https://pedestrianobservations.com/2019/11/18/what-does-private-affluence-public-squalor-mean/

Prenzler, T. (2021). Grey corruption issues in the public sector. *Journal of Criminological Research, Policy and Practice, 7*(2), 137–149.

Prenzler, T., & Wilson, E. (2019). The Ipswich (Queensland) safe city program: An evaluation. *Security Journal, 32*(2), 137–152.

Prenzler, T., Cairns, N., Moir, E., & Rayment-McHugh, S. (2022). *Nambour community safety review: Stage 1 report.* Sunshine Coast Council and University of the Sunshine Coast. file:///C:/Users/User/Downloads/Nambour%20Community%20Safety%20Review%20-%20Stage%201%20Report.pdf

Sampson, R., Raudenbush, S., & Earls, F. (1997). Neighbourhoods and violent crime: A multilevel study of collective efficacy. *Science, 277*(5328), 918–924.

Shearing, C., & Stenning, P. (1981). Modern private security: Its growth and implication. In N. Morris & M. Tonry (Eds.), *Crime and Justice: An Annual Review of Research* (pp. 193–245). University of Chicago Press.

Sherman, L., Gartin, P., & Buerger, M. (1989). Hot spots of predatory crime: Routine activities and the criminology of place. *Criminology, 27*(1), 27–55.

Shinn, M. (2010). Homelessness, poverty and social exclusion in the United States and Europe. *European Journal of Homelessness, 4*(December), 19–44.

Tax Justice Network. (2023). *State of tax justice 2023.* https://taxjustice.net/reports/the-state-of-tax-justice-2023/

United Nations. (2023, May 2). *Stamping out corruption can give SDGs $3 trillion boost.* https://www.un.org/en/desa/stamping-out-corruption-can-give-sdgs-3-trillion-boost

Varela, P. (2015, December 9). *Brief: Progressive and regressive taxes.* https://www.austaxpolicy.com/what-are-progressive-and-regressive-taxes/#:~:text=In%20simple%20terms%2C%20a%20progressive,income%20decreases%20as%20income%20increases

Wilson, J., & Kelling, G. (1982). 'Broken windows': The police and neighbourhood safety. *Atlantic Monthly, 249*(3), 29–38.

CHAPTER 2

Creating Defensible Spaces and Designing Out Opportunities for Crime

Abstract This chapter outlines a best practice framework for reducing or eliminating public crime and disorder problems. Situational crime prevention and CPTED (Crime Prevention Through Environmental Design) provide core concepts, including defensible space, territoriality, guardianship and assisting compliance. The idea of an enforcement pyramid also aids planning. Additional applied theories include community policing, reassurance policing, quality-of-life policing and third-party policing. Social contract theory and systematic problem solving (or 'problem-oriented policing') constitute overarching frameworks. These theories are developed from research on what does and doesn't work in crime prevention. Consequently, they provide important starting points and a shared language for developing strategies that are most likely to be effective, subject to local conditions. The chapter includes a set of intervention case studies in the areas of lighting, road and alley closures, public housing layouts and security upgrades in order to illustrate these principles at work in real life.

Keywords Situational prevention · CPTED · Social contract · Crime triangle

17

T. Prenzler, *Preventing Crime and Disorder in Public Places*, Crime Prevention and Security Management, https://doi.org/10.1007/978-3-031-63764-3_2

SITUATIONAL CRIME PREVENTION

The previous chapter outlined the diagnostic power of rationale choice theory and routine activity theory in explaining key factors that drive crime in public places. Situational crime prevention then provides the best framework for matching diagnoses to preventive interventions. Clarke (1997, p. 4) provides the following definition:

> Situational prevention comprises opportunity-reducing measures that (1) are directed at highly specific forms of crime, (2) involve the management, design or manipulation of the immediate environment in as systematic and permanent way as possible, (3) make crime more difficult and risky, or less rewarding and excusable as judged by a wide range of offenders.

These 'opportunity-reducing measures' can be actioned through 25 techniques, grouped under five strategic areas: 'increase the effort', 'increase the risks', 'reduce the rewards', 'reduce provocations' and 'remove excuses' (see Table 2.1).

These approaches can also be structured in terms of a hierarchy of 'hard' and 'soft' approaches (Prenzler & Wilson, 2017, p. 64). Harder methods involve various forms of 'target hardening', denial of access and threats of arrest and punishment. Examples include locks, fences, barriers, street closures, security guards and police. Softer approaches 'assist compliance' by communicating rules, reducing provocations and temptations and making it easy for people to obey rules—helping obviate the need for law enforcement. This approach also activates the situational concepts of 'remove excuses', 'alert conscience' and 'post instructions'. Examples of facilitating compliance include the following:

- Providing entertainment when people are queuing reduces irritability and conflict.
- Providing food and entertainment at licensed premises reduces boredom, intoxication and the likelihood of violence.
- Visible, accessible, free public toilets help prevent public urination.
- The availability of rubbish bins helps prevent littering.
- Frequent and clear speed limit signs help prevent inadvertent speeding and remind wilful speedsters of the law and their obligations.

Table 2.1 The 25 techniques of situational crime prevention

Increase the effort	Increase the risks	Reduce the rewards	Reduce provocations	Remove excuses
1. Target harden • Steering column locks and immobilisers • Anti-robbery screens • Tamper-proof packaging	6. Extend guardianship • Take routine precautions: go out in group at night, leave signs of occupancy, carry phone • "Cocoon" neighborhood watch	11. Conceal targets • Off-street parking • Gender-neutral phone directories • Unmarked bullion trucks	16. Reduce frustrations and stress • Efficient queues and polite service • Expanded seating • Soothing music/muted lights	21. Set rules • Rental agreements • Harassment codes • Hotel registration
2. Control access to facilities • Entry phones • Electronic card access • Baggage screening	7. Assist natural surveillance • Improved street lighting • Defensible space design • Support whistleblowers	12. Remove targets • Removable car radio • Women's refuges • Pre-paid cards for pay phones	17. Avoid disputes • Separate enclosures for rival soccer fans • Reduce crowding in pubs • Fixed cab fares	22. Post instructions • "No Parking" • "Private Property" • "Extinguish camp fires"
3. Screen exits • Ticket needed for exit • Export documents • Electronic merchandise tags	8. Reduce anonymity • Taxi driver IDs • "How's my driving?" decals • School uniforms	13. Identify property • Property marking • Vehicle licensing and parts marking • Cattle branding	18. Reduce emotional arousal • Controls on violent pornography • Enforce good behavior on soccer field • Prohibit racial slurs	23. Alert conscience • Roadside speed display boards • Signatures for customs declarations • "Shoplifting is stealing"

(continued)

Table 2.1 (continued)

Increase the effort	Increase the risks	Reduce the rewards	Reduce provocations	Remove excuses
4. Deflect offenders • Street closures • Separate bathrooms for women • Disperse pubs	9. Utilize place managers • CCTV for double-deck buses • Two clerks for convenience stores • Reward vigilance	14. Disrupt markets • Monitor pawn shops • Controls on classified ads • License street vendors	19. Neutralize peer pressure • "Idiots drink and drive" • "It's OK to say No" • Disperse troublemakers at school	24. Assist compliance • Easy library checkout • Public lavatories • Litter bins
5. Control tools/weapons • "Smart" guns • Disabling stolen cell phones • Restrict spray paint sales to juveniles	10. Strengthen formal surveillance • Red light cameras • Burglar alarms • Security guards	15. Deny benefits • Ink merchandise tags • Graffiti cleaning • Speed humps	20. Discourage imitation • Rapid repair of vandalism • V-chips in TVs • Censor details of modus operandi	25. Control drugs and alcohol • Breathalyzers in pubs • Server intervention • Alcohol-free events

Source Cornish and Clarke (2003, p. 90). Used with permission

In between hard and soft approaches, intermediate opportunity-reducing measures include 'denying benefits', 'deflecting offenders' and 'assisting natural surveillance'. As shown in Table 2.1, these can involve interventions such as rapid removal of graffiti to reduce offender gratification, reducing vehicle access points to crime targets and clearing clutter to improve the visibility of potential offenders.

This idea of a hierarchy of approaches overlaps with another very useful crime prevention planning framework: an 'enforcement pyramid' (Fig. 2.1). At the base of the pyramid, compliance is encouraged through communication, assistance and warnings, supported by the social contract (further below). If these fail, then interventions need to be escalated through more painful measures such as fines, licence revocations and evictions; with persistent non-compliance justifying the much more intrusive interventions of arrest and incarceration. However, the latter need not entail simply warehousing prisoners but should include a variety of productive supervision, rehabilitation and reintegration management options (Baker & McKillop, 2017; Prenzler et al., 2023). Although not shown in Fig. 2.1, an enforcement period also has scope for victim compensation and victim–offender mediation, which can reduce the harm experienced from crime and help prevent re-offending.

Prison
Supervision
Disqualification
Fine
Banning/eviction
Curfew
Naming and shaming
Warning
Assistance
Communication

Fig. 2.1 A sample enforcement pyramid 1992 (*Source* adapted from Ayres and Braithwaite [, p. 35])

The 25 situational techniques are not intended to be applied indiscriminately. The focus is on fitting interventions to specific situations, and this can only be determined through primary research. In that regard, the techniques provide a set of options for consideration, but only a few might be of direct relevance to a particular crime problem. From that perspective, Clarke sets out five stages—based on an 'action research' process—required for the implementation of a situational prevention project (1997, p. 15):

1. Collection of data about the nature and dimensions of the specific crime problem;
2. Analysis of the situational conditions that permit or facilitate the commission of the crime in question;
3. Systematic study of possible means of blocking opportunities for these particular crimes, including analysis of costs;
4. Implementation of the most promising, feasible and economic measures;
5. Monitoring of results and dissemination of experience.

Enhancing Guardianship: Operationalising the Crime Triangle

The previous chapter briefly described the crime triangle, which sets out the most basic ingredients for crime: an offender, a victim and a location. Modifying the relationships within the triangle in the right way should reduce crime. We also saw in Chapter 1 that negligent management can be a major facilitator of crime problems. Consequently, responsible 'place management' is arguably the most important factor in creating safe places (Eck et al., 2007, p. 240). This can be explicated in part through the complete crime triangle as a preventive tool, shown in Fig. 2.2. The three countervailing elements, added to each side, show potential roles for human agency in reducing opportunities (Clarke & Eck, 2003).

A 'manager' has responsibility for conduct in a designated space, 'such as a bus conductor or teacher at a school' (Clarke & Eck, 2003, p. 27). Managers have a central role in crime diagnostics and the introduction of situational strategies (Table 2.1). A 'handler' is someone who has a relationship with a potential offender and can exercise influence

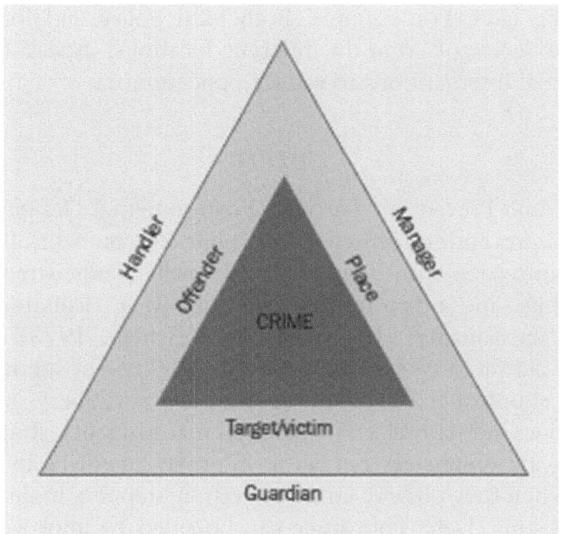

Fig. 2.2   The complete crime triangle 2003 (*Source* Clarke and Eck [, p. 9].
Used with permission)

or control over their conduct. Handlers include friends on a night out,
parents in public places and other types of escorts. A handler could be a
parole officer supervising offenders engaged in community service work.
'Capable guardians' are 'usually people protecting their own belongings'
or those of other people (p. 26) and include both informal guardians,
such as bystanders or shop staff, and formal guardians, such as police or
security officers. It could be argued that in some situations managers and
handlers can also act as guardians and vice-versa. So, when thinking about
crime and disorder in public places we need to first ask about who is in
charge and what measures they are taking to reduce crime opportunities.
Is there more they could be doing? The answer is probably 'yes'.

This approach also follows from the fact that crime does not occur
evenly across people and places. The more that crime is concentrated
in specific locations—such as 'hot spots'—or amongst specific types of
victims the more likely it is that focused interventions will have a preventive effect (Hayes & Prenzler, 2020, pp. 88–92). When thinking about
crime and place, government authorities always have some kind of direct
place management responsibilities, including setting the legal framework

and enforcing laws. For example, both local police and local councils should assess levels of crime in different locations, especially in public places, and trial interventions to reduce opportunities.

CPTED

CPTED—Crime Prevention Through Environmental Design—is a form of situational prevention focused on the built environment. The CPTED method is concerned with designing open malls, parks, streets, schools, office buildings and other locations in ways that facilitate 'defensible space' and 'territoriality' (Crowe, 1991; Newman, 1973). Defensible space can be activated by strategies such as visibility—by methods such as decluttering shopfronts and trimming trees and shrubbery on pathways. Clear sight lines aid natural surveillance so that residents, shoppers, business owners and employees can act as informal guardians by contacting authorities when they observe crime or even by stepping in directly to de-escalate problems. Defensible space can be aided by improved lighting, demarcation of 'public, semi-private and private' zones, and with user-friendly target-hardening devices such as entry phones. Territoriality refers to having a stake in the welfare of a location—by feeling like a valued tenant or employee, for example—and willingly contributing to collective guardianship. 'Image' involves the aesthetics of a location. Places that are attractive and well-maintained signal the presence of occupants with a commitment to protection.

The CPTED focus on place incorporates the concept of place management, highlighting the responsibilities of property owners and managers for the safety and security of tenants, employees and visitors—in part through applying CPTED principles (Mihinjac & Reynald, 2017). 'Separating legitimate and non-legitimate' users of space is a classic CPTED strategy that makes use of the situational techniques of 'control access to facilities' and 'deflect offenders'. Examples of entry (and exit) control include concierges, ID checks, swipe cards and tickets. Offenders can be deflected away from targets through techniques such as road closures and chill-out zones. 'Activity generators' are events and facilities that attract legitimate users who can act as guardians. Examples include playgrounds, street theatre, buskers, markets and evening and weekend room rentals in schools.

Table 2.2 Sample CPTED audit matrix with CPTED principles

Audit category	Key CPTED principles
Lighting	Surveillance, Access Control, Target Hardening, Safety
Sightlines	Surveillance, Guardianship, Target Hardening, Safety
Ownership of Space	Territoriality, Activity Support, Guardianship, Social Cohesion, Safety, Image Maintenance, Target Hardening
Perceptions of Crime and Safety	Access Control, Guardianship, Safety
Signage/CCTV	Surveillance, Image Maintenance, Target Hardening
Movement	Access Control, Activity Support, Image Maintenance, Target Hardening, Social Cohesion, Connectivity
Landscaping	Activity Support, Image Maintenance, Target Hardening, Safety
Space Use—Use Mix and Activity Generation	Surveillance, Guardianship, Access Control, Activity Support, Target Hardening, Social Cohesion, Connectivity
Maintenance and Management	Image Maintenance, Target Hardening, Connectivity

Source Prenzler et al. (2022, pp. 55–56)

CPTED audits, involving physical inspections and stakeholder consultation, are a key tool for identifying aspects of settings that can be modified to reduce opportunities for crime (Prenzler et al., 2022, chapter 3). A sample CPTED audit matrix with nine core categories is provided in Table 2.2. This instrument uses a five-point scale to rate 106 features of the environment associated with factors that facilitate or inhibit crime and disorder and feelings of safety or insecurity.

PROBLEM SOLVING AND COMMUNITY ENGAGEMENT

The principles outlined so far resonate with the idea of a general 'problem-solving approach' to crime reduction through consultation, diagnostics, intervention and testing. One version of this is Clarke's five steps of situational analysis and intervention (above). It has also been formulated within a 'problem-oriented policing' (POP) framework in terms of four steps in the SARA model: 'Scan, Analyse, Respond, Assess' (Eck & Spelman, 1987). This includes continuous monitoring and improvement. There are also strong overlaps here with a variety of other prevention-focused frameworks, summarised briefly below.

- *Community policing* posits the idea that police cannot reduce crime on their own. They need to work closely with their local communities and share responsibility for crime prevention (Trojanowicz & Bucqueroux, 1990). Initiatives within this framework have included consultative committees, and public opinion and experience surveys, regarding crime problems and priorities. Community policing incorporated the neighbourhood watch movement and encouraged police foot patrols and shopfronts, crime awareness programs and security advice services.
- *Reassurance policing* focuses on public insecurity about crime, arguing that police should do more to make people feel safe. Specifically, it proposed police target 'signal crimes', which trigger fear of crime, and activate 'control signals', which indicate that legitimate and capable guardians are present (Innes & Fielding, 2002). Examples include graffiti removal and visible police patrols.
- Similarly, *quality-of-life policing*, based on broken windows theory (Chapter 1), argues that signs of disorder signal the absence of guardians, deter law-abiding persons and attract offenders (Bratton, 2015; Kelling & Coles, 1998). Authorities should work together to reduce signs of neglect and target what are often considered minor crimes, such as public nuisance offences. Preventing minor crimes should make people feel safer and go out more. Managed properly, this approach is potentially beneficial to offenders, especially young offenders experimenting with crime, in keeping them off the path to a criminal lifestyle.
- According to *third-party policing*, when owners and managers of premises fail to act to reduce crime problems, government regulatory authorities should use incentives and deterrents, such as the renewal or revocation of an operating licence, to provoke compliance (Mazerolle & Ransley, 2005). One example of the application of third-party policing has been with rental houses that are used as neighbourhood drug sales points (pp. 104–105). Another example is threats by liquor licensing authorities to remove licences and shut down pubs and clubs if they do not comply with responsible serving

practices (see Chapter 6, Reducing Intoxication and Alcohol-related Crime in Entertainment Precincts).

SOCIAL CONTRACT THEORY AND PROCEDURAL JUSTICE

Chapter 1 described problems of crime and feelings of insecurity in public places as symptoms of a failed social contract between citizens and politicians. Operationalising the social contract means getting the social justice and procedural justice settings right for optimal crime reduction. This involves three key conditions. In the first instance, the legal framework for crime and regulatory offences needs to be democratically determined. This means that the law needs to be legitimate by reflecting the will of the people through an open and fair consultative process, with a legislature that is elected through free and fair elections, with comprehensive governmental transparency and accountability, an independent media to challenge government decisions and an independent judiciary to determine cases free of prejudice or undue influence (Prenzler, 2021, chapter 1). Secondly, as the gatekeepers of the criminal justice system, police need to act independently of politics and follow procedural justice standards in enforcing the law. Procedural justice principles—emphasising 'voice, neutrality, respect and trust' (Tyler, 2003)—constitute an essential requirement for public confidence in, and cooperation with, police (Bolger & Walters, 2019).

The third condition is that citizens need to have a deep 'stake in conformity' (Toby, 1957)—in living within a democratic state that provides equality of opportunity and widespread prosperity. This entails 'removing the excuses' for crime through access to employment, a living wage and adequate health and welfare services. From the perspective of criminological 'strain theory', this means minimising the stressors on people that can motivate crime (Bull, 2020, p. 216). In other words, in theory, this removes the motive to commit a crime out of 'need'. For those who commit offences, health and social deficits need to be addressed through access to therapies and reintegration programs. This approach resonates with the idea of government obligations to observe human rights (Prenzler, 2021, pp. 11–12), including a broad concept of 'the responsibility to protect' (Bellamy & Dunne, 2016). As one example, in central business districts, where disadvantaged persons often congregate and become both victims and offenders in street crimes, authorities need to provide adequate housing and support as part of a comprehensive program of welfare and safety.

SAMPLE STRATEGIES IN ACTION

The following section of this chapter provides a small set of examples of situationally based measures where case studies provide evidence of success. These are in the areas of lighting, road and alleyway closures and housing project security. The main situational strategies illustrated in the case studies are improving guardianship, utilising place managers, reducing anonymity, limiting access and escape, deflecting offenders and target hardening.

Lighting

Lighting can help guardians to see potential offenders and potential victims at night. It can help prevent offenders from hiding. There is a body of evidence that supports a positive relationship between quality street lighting, reduced crime and disorder and enhanced feelings of safety (Painter, 1994; Seifi et al., 2023; Welsh & Farrington, 2008). Improvements can also occur during daylight hours, due in part to increased community ownership of space through a process referred to as a 'diffusion of benefits' or a 'halo effect' (Clarke, 1997, p. 31). One recent example of improved street lighting involved public housing developments in New York City. The program was associated with a reduction of 36% in more serious 'index' crimes occurring outdoors at night—including homicides, felony assaults, robberies and motor vehicle theft (Chalfin et al., 2019, 17). The financial benefit-to-cost ratio was put at 4 to 1 (p. 21). Two other examples follow in more detail.

The Kansas City Relighting Program represents an early example of improving street lighting as a way to reduce crime. It involved a partnership between the Kansas City Department of Public Works and the US government National Institute for Law Enforcement and Criminal Justice (Wright et al., 1974). The latter had been interested in exploring the relationship between street lighting and crime, and the Kansas City government agreed to participate and accept a proposed evaluation process. A grant was provided to support the program, with the evaluation carried out by the University of Michigan. Rising crime rates in the city provided the context for the project. Work began with exploratory studies of crime locations and optimal levels of lighting. A range of commercial and residential areas were selected for lighting upgrades. The focus was on violent 'street crime' occurring at night, especially robbery. The 'relighting' process was described as follows (Wright et al., 1974, p. 1):

> Between October 1971 and March 1972, 1800 mercury and sodium streetlights were installed in approximately 500 blocks in the downtown business district and a mixed residential/commercial neighbourhood. These lights replaced the older incandescent illumination in these blocks.

The project evaluation was complex, with diverse findings. The main positive impact was in the target area of violent crime occurring at night, mainly robbery. In the 12 months prior to the lighting upgrade, night-time street robberies had increased by 32% in the target blocks (Wright et al., 1974, p. 49). In the 12 months post-installation, robberies in this category decreased by 52%, from 67 to 32. Street assaults at night had increased by 40% prior to the upgrade and then decreased by 41% from 37 to 22. There was a small reduction in robbery in the 'non-relit blocks' and a very small increase in assaults. There did not appear to be any displacement of robberies to relit streets during the day (temporal displacement) and also 'non-street locations' (such as alleyways, parks and schoolyards) in relit blocks (spatial displacement). However, there were large increases in assaults in these areas (67% for night-time non-street locations, from 21 to 35, and 78% for daytime street locations, from 21 to 35). Overall, despite these negatives, the researchers saw the project as a success: 'The crimes of primary interest in this study—night street crimes of violence, which are the crimes that most terrorise people—showed dramatic and significant responsiveness to upgraded street lighting' (p. 58).

In the early 1990s, the housing estate of Dudley in England experienced a major crime problem, including high levels of fear of crime. About 70% of crime occurred after daylight hours. In the Dudley Project, the local authority upgraded street lighting across 1.5 kilometres of roads (Painter & Farrington, 1997). The sodium high-pressure white lights installed at the experimental site doubled the amount of light, greatly improving natural surveillance.

The project evaluation involved surveys of residents conducted one year before and one year after installation. A similar area, physically and demographically, was adopted as a comparison site. In the experimental site, there was a 23% reduction in reported victimisation from 42.0%

of respondents to 32.3%. The control site saw victimisation fall by 3%, from 39.1% to 38.0%. In terms of the incidence of crime, there was a 41% reduction at the experimental site from 114.8 crimes per 100 households to 68.0. For the control site, crime fell 15% from 82.1 incidents per 100 households to 69.8. In the experimental site, the overall reduction included a 38% drop in burglaries, a 39% drop in 'outside theft/vandalism', a 49% drop in 'vehicle crime' and a 41% drop in 'personal crime' (p. 218). A financial cost–benefit analysis found that in one year the project had stopped 641 crimes, resulting in a financial saving of £558,415 against installation and operating costs (Painter & Farrington, 2001). Despite these achievements, a disappointing aspect of the study was that Dudley residents' feelings of insecurity saw little change (Painter & Farrington, 1997; but see Painter, 1994 on improved feelings of safety in other case studies).

Road and Alleyway Closures

Multiple roadways provide easy access to crime targets and quick escape routes. Alleyways can also provide hiding places for assailants and access to the backs of shops and residences by burglars. To counter this problem, roads can be blocked off permanently or for limited periods and alleys can be gated with selected access via locks. Program evaluations have generally shown positive outcomes (e.g., Clarke, 2004; Sidebottom et al., 2018).

'Operation Cul-de-Sac' in Los Angeles in the early 1990s is an outstanding example. The police-initiated program involved restricted vehicle and pedestrian access to hot spots for gang shootings, mainly via locked fences and large planter boxes across 14 streets, involving ten city blocks (Lasley, 1996). The street closures were associated with large reductions in drive-by shootings and fatalities, with no evidence of displacement. Substantial reductions also occurred in rapes, assaults and robberies. Drive-by shootings recorded by police fell from 38 in 1989, the year before the intervention, to one in 1990, the first year of the intervention (−95%). Furthermore, the number of murders had averaged 5 + per year prior to the intervention, and five in 1989, with one murder recorded in the following two years (−90%). Residents were frustrated with a lack of consultation about the project but felt much safer and went out more often. However, the project fell apart when police withdrew their support. Rates for most crimes returned to normal and the homicide rate rose above the pre-intervention rate.

A somewhat similar program in the early 1980s in the Finsbury Park area of London addressed the problem of street prostitution—or 'curb crawling'—and associated issues of harassment, crime and traffic congestion. Following the failure of police crackdowns through intensified arrests, meetings between police, local residents and the local council led to an agreement to close selected roads. The initiative led to 'a remarkable transformation ... Soliciting and curb crawling virtually disappeared, and the area was transformed from a noisy and hazardous "red light" district into a relatively tranquil residential area', with no evidence of displacement (Matthews, 1997, p. 78).

Housing Project Layouts and Security Upgrades

In 'a tale of two projects', CPTED pioneer Oscar Newman (1973) described crime and disorder problems in two high-rise public housing projects in New York City. The van Dyke complex had recorded felony and misdemeanour offences approximately 1.5 times those of the nearby Brownsville complex (p. 47). Robbery rates at van Dyke were almost twice those of Brownsville. Newman observed that the demographics of the residents were largely the same. Consequently, the most likely explanation for the variation lay in the different building designs. Van Dyke was characterised by concealed paths, high-load lifts (elevators) and anonymous corridors, and there was a lack of observable street entrances. In contract, Brownsville was structured around observable zones, with small lifts and small vestibules, and there were observable street entrances. Newman hypothesised that the layout of the high-crime van Dyke project created high levels of anonymity, which facilitated offender entry and escape. In Brownsville, the more intimate and restricted spaces meant that neighbours could identify each other and challenge strangers. The van Dyke project also had problems of high maintenance, high tenant turnover and lower tenant involvement in governance compared to Brownsville, which had a more stable and involved community.

A number of features of a crime reduction program in the Mitchellhill public housing estate in Glasgow, Scotland, also involved enhanced guardianship and reduced anonymity (Davidson & Farr, 1994). These changes also helped reduce resident alienation. In this case, the situational strategy of 'utilise place managers' was also prominent. Introduced in 1989 by the local authority, with police support, the program included the following specific initiatives:

- an on-site manager and assistant,
- 12 building concierges who provided 24-hour security-oriented services to residents,
- security hardware such as solid doors with barrel locks rekeyed for new tenants,
- improved lighting,
- CCTV,
- controlled entry to foyers,
- removal of internal landing doors that provided hiding places,
- increased police patrols,
- a 'multi-watch' system for residents to report issues to the concierges or police,
- improvements to the attractiveness of the estate with renovations and provision of furnished flats, and
- tenant representation on the tenant selection committee.

Some target hardening and enlarged formal surveillance strategies were clearly in place here but controlled entry to foyers and removal of landing doors also helped reduce anonymity. Formal guardians were also able to identify legitimate users and challenge illegitimate users.

An evaluation reported that the total number of police-recorded crimes fell by 62% from 141 to 53 in the 15 months following the roll out of the program (Davidson & Farr, 1994, p. 26). In the same period, burglaries were reduced by 71% and theft of vehicles and theft from vehicles reduced by 72%. Large reductions in maintenance costs, mainly associated with vandalism, were also recorded; along with increased demand for flats, increased occupancy and increased rental income. Crime rates remained stable over the same period in a nearby comparable area.

CONCLUSION

This chapter summarised major theoretical frameworks useful for designing effective crime reduction programs for public spaces. These frameworks provide concepts and language for crime prevention planning. They also provide a set of strategies which should be considered as applicable depending on the nature of the crime problem under consideration. Situational prevention and CPTED stand out as approaches that have direct relevance to public places with a very high probability of success if correctly implemented—especially where enhanced guardianship is involved. More broadly, a systematic data-based problem-solving strategy, founded on the social contract and procedural justice, provides for an overarching best practice approach.

REFERENCES

Ayres, I., & Braithwaite, J. (1992). *Responsive regulation: Transcending the deregulation debate.* Oxford University Press.

Baker, M., & McKillop, N. (2017). Offender management and rehabilitation. In T. Prenzler (Ed.), *Understanding crime prevention: The case study approach* (pp. 27–43). Australian Academic Press.

Bellamy, A., & Dunne, T. (2016). *The Oxford handbook of the responsibility to protect.* Oxford University Press.

Bolger, P., & Walters, G. (2019). The relationship between police procedural justice, police legitimacy, and people's willingness to cooperate with law enforcement: A meta-analysis. *Journal of Criminal Justice, 60*(January–February), 93–99.

Bratton, W. (2015). *Broken windows and quality-of-life policing in New York City.* http://www.nyc.gov/html/nypd/downloads/pdf/analysis_and_planning/qol.pdf

Bull, M. (2020). Social explanations. In H. Hayes & T. Prenzler (Eds.), *An introduction to crime and criminology* (pp. 210–227). Pearson.

Chalfin, A., Hansen, B., Lerner, J., & Parker, L. (2019). *Reducing crime through environmental design: Evidence from a randomized experiment of street lighting in New York City.* University of Chicago.

Clarke, R. (1997). Introduction. In R. Clarke (Ed.), *Situational crime prevention: Successful case studies* (pp. 1–43). Harrow and Heston.

Clarke, R. (2004). *Closing streets and alleys to reduce crime: Should you go down this road?* US Department of Justice, Office of Community Oriented Policing Services.

Clarke, R., & Eck, J. (2003). *Become a problem solving crime analysis in 55 small steps.* University College London.

Crowe, T. (1991). *Crime prevention through environmental design: Applications of architectural design and space management concepts.* Butterworth-Heinemann.

Davidson, J., & Farr, J. (1994). Mitchellhill estate: Estate-based management (concierge) initiative. In S. Osborn (Ed.), *Housing safe communities: An evaluation of recent initiatives* (pp. 22–33). Safe Neighbourhoods Unit.

Eck, J., & Spelman, W. (1987). *Problem-solving: Problem-oriented policing in Newport News.* United States National Institute of Justice.

Eck, J., Clarke, R., & Guerette, R. (2007). Risky facilities. *Crime Prevention Studies, 21*, 225–264.

Hayes, H., & Prenzler, T. (2020). Victim and offender characteristics. In H. Hayes & T. Prenzler (Eds.), *An introduction to crime and criminology* (pp. 80–100). Pearson.

Innes, M., & Fielding, N. (2002). From community to communicative policing: 'Signal crimes' and the problem of public reassurance. *Sociological Research Online, 7*(2), 1–22.

Kelling, G., & Coles, C. (1998). *Fixing broken windows: Reducing crime and restoring order in our communities.* Simon and Schuster.

Lasley, J. (1996). *Using traffic barriers to 'design out' crime: A program evaluation of LAPD's operation Cul-de-sac.* US Department of Justice.

Matthews, R. (1997). Developing more effective strategies for curbing prostitution. In R. Clarke (Ed.), *Situational crime prevention: Successful case studies* (pp. 74–82). Harrow and Heston.

Mazerolle, L., & Ransley, J. (2005). *Third party policing.* Cambridge University Press.

Mihinjac, M., & Reynald, D. (2017). Crime prevention through environmental design: Evolution, theory and practice. In T. Prenzler (Ed.), *Understanding crime prevention: The Case study approach* (pp. 89–105). Australian Academic Press.

Newman, O. (1973). *Defensible space: Crime prevention through environmental design.* Collier Books.

Painter, K. (1994). The impact of street lighting on crime, fear, and pedestrian street use. *Security Journal, 5*(3), 116–124.

Painter, K., & Farrington, D. (1997). The crime reducing effect of improved street lighting: The Dudley Project. In R. Clarke (Ed.), *Situational crime prevention: Successful case studies* (pp. 209–226). Harrow and Heston.

Painter, K., & Farrington, D. (2001). The financial benefits of improved street lighting, based on crime reduction. *Lighting Research Technology, 33*(1), 3–12.

Prenzler, T. (2021). *Ethics and accountability in criminal justice.* Australian Academic Press.

Prenzler, T., & Wilson, E. (2017). The evolution of situational crime prevention. In T. Prenzler (Ed.), *Understanding crime prevention: The case study approach* (pp. 73–88). Australian Academic Press.

Prenzler, T., Cairns, N., Moir, E., & Rayment-McHugh, S. (2022). *Nambour community safety review: Stage 1 report.* Sunshine Coast Council and The University of the Sunshine Coast. https://research.usc.edu.au/esploro/outputs/report/Nambour-Community-Safety-Review-Stage-1/99680498102621?institution=61USC_INST#file-0

Prenzler, T., McKillop, N., Rayment-McHugh, S., & Christensen, L. (2023). Best practice in sexual offender rehabilitation and reintegration programs. *Journal of Criminological Research, Policy and Practice, 9*(3/4), 207–221.

Seifi, M., Cozens, P., Reynald, D., Haron, S., & Abdullah, A. (2023). How effective are residential CCTV systems? Evaluating the impact of natural versus mechanical surveillance on house break-ins and theft in hotspots of Penang Island, Malaysia. *Security Journal, 36*(1), 49–81.

Sidebottom, A., Tilley, N., Johnson, S., Bowers, K., Tompson, L., Thornton, A., & Bullock, K. (2018). Gating alleys to reduce crime: A meta-analysis and realist synthesis. *Justice Quarterly., 35*(1), 55–86.

Toby, J. (1957). Social disorganization and stake in conformity: Complementary factors in the predatory behavior of hoodlums. *The Journal of Criminal Law, Criminology, and Police Science, 48*(1), 12–17.

Trojanowicz, R., & Bucqueroux, B. (1990). *Community policing: A contemporary perspective.* Anderson.

Tyler, T. (2003). Procedural justice, legitimacy, and effective rule of law. *Crime and Justice: A Review of Research, 30*, 283–357.

Welsh, B., & Farrington, D. (2008). *Effects of improved street lighting on crime.* Campbell Collaboration.

Wright, R., Heilweil, M., Pelletier, P., & Dickinson, K. (1974). *The Impact of street lighting on street crime.* University of Michigan.

CHAPTER 3

Combining Police and Security Patrols with Welfare Services

Abstract Police patrols are often put forward as an essential form of guardianship in public places. The ideal contemporary model that is often advocated involves officers on foot, in locations where crime and disorder are concentrated, linked to a CCTV system. This chapter reviews the evidence in this area, emphasising the importance of community consultation and tailor-made applications, along with the potential value of police and security patrols with a strong welfare role—including a co-responding role with specialist personnel to address issues of mental illness, drug dependence and homelessness. Examples of diverse types of patrol-based programs reviewed in the chapter include the Newcastle upon Tyne City Centre Partnership Security Initiative, Indigenous Night Patrols, Cairns Street Chaplains and the Adachi Ward Beautiful Windows Movement in Tokyo.

Keywords Foot patrols · Partnerships · CCTV · Welfare services

© The Author(s), under exclusive license to Springer Nature Switzerland AG 2024
T. Prenzler, *Preventing Crime and Disorder in Public Places*, Crime Prevention and Security Management,
https://doi.org/10.1007/978-3-031-63764-3_3

Foot Patrols

The deployment of police officers in public places to prevent crime and anti-social behaviour is a common preference of citizens. Patrols entail an application of the reassurance policing agenda, discussed in Chapter 1 and operationalisation of the situational prevention concepts of 'extend guardianship' and 'strengthen formal surveillance'. Patrols represent a democratic response to public expectations about visible authority and protection (Crawford et al., 2005). Concentrating patrols on crime map hot spots has been referred to as 'putting cops on dots' (in Ariel et al., 2016, p. 281).

Foot patrols in the form of 'beat policing' was the original form of uniformed professional policing that developed in the late-eighteenth and early-nineteenth centuries in the British Isles, adopted from earlier night watchmen models and subsequently adopted around the world. The core model was very simple (Drew & Prenzler, 2015, p. 8):

> Officers patrolled the streets on foot in shifts within a designated beat area. The visible presence of the police was meant to deter crime, and if that failed they provided a rapid response to protect the victim and arrest the offender where appropriate. Citizens who saw a crime in progress, or were attacked or threatened themselves, could alert the patrol officers who were expected to respond with all speed.

The ideals of the New Police were summed up in what are referred to as 'Peel's principles', which are still highly relevant today. The principles focus on the prevention of crime and disorder as more important goals than solving crime or arresting offenders. Police were meant to obtain public support, work as much as possible with their communities, use force as an absolute last resort and provide general assistance. According to Richard Mayne, a co-commissioner of the London Metropolitan Police, the success of the police would be measured in terms of 'the protection of life and property, the preservation of public tranquillity, and the absence of crime' (in Drew & Prenzler, 2015, p. 9).

One of the major criticisms of modern policing, as it evolved in the twentieth century, was that officers preferred to patrol in air-conditioned motor vehicles and arrest suspects. As a consequence, they frequently lost touch with their local constituencies (Trojanowicz & Bucqueroux, 1990). Putting community policing and reassurance policing into action often involves putting officers back on the streets, where they are more notice-able and can interact with citizens. From a liberal democratic perspective, the role of beat officers in deterring crime and providing assistance is preferred over aggressive arrest-focused strategies, and the absence of police in public places appears as a source of major dissatisfaction. For example, a survey in London found that 65% of respondents rated 'more police around on foot' as the type of crime prevention initiative most likely to increase security in their area (MORI, 2005, p. 1; see Metcalfe & Pickett, 2018; Wakefield, 2006, pp. 22–24). In that regard, a recent report on policing in the United Kingdom by the Police Foundation (2020) emphasised a mismatch in policy between police priorities and public priorities, as evidenced by focus group studies. This was manifested most noticeably in the decline of a visible police presence, and a strong sense of disorder and danger in public spaces (p. 54):

> the desire for a greater police presence was expressed most often in the context of a general sense of 'deterioration' in the quality and atmosphere of familiar local public spaces (such as town centres, parks and shopping precincts). In many locations respondents identified empty shops, civic disrepair, street homelessness and visible drug and alcohol misuse as signs of a local 'turn for the worse' and saw these changes as indicators of increased threat. The instinctive response to this increased sense of nearby malignancy was often to call for a greater deterrent police presence.

The final report by the Police Foundation (2022) identified a correlation between fluctuations in the numbers of officers engaged in community policing in England and Wales, the visibility of police on foot and public confidence in the police and local authorities to deal with crime (p. 51).

The Impacts of Police Foot Patrols

Wakefield's (2006) review of 13 police foot patrol programs found they could positively influence citizens' feelings of safety, consistent with the reassurance policing and quality-of-life policing agendas (Chapter 2). In terms of the community policing agenda, they also tended to include varying degrees of community consultation and involvement, including 'community meetings, committees and "proactive contacts" such as door-to-door visits' (p. 12). Police simply being visible on the ground represents the least sophisticated and least satisfactory type of program (Wakefield, 2006).

In terms of reducing crime, police foot patrols have shown mixed results, with some studies indicating reductions and some not (e.g., Braga et al., 2019; Ratcliffe et al., 2015; Wakefield, 2006). The initial introduction of foot patrols and shopfronts can increase levels of crime reporting and detection (Taylor & Charlton, 2005), although it should support long-term declines in crime. Pioneering modern projects in the United States—in Newark and Flint—included examples of increased satisfaction with police, reduced fear of crime and reduced crime (Pate et al., 1985; Trojanowicz, 1982). A fairly recent evaluation of the Dayton Foot Patrol Program in Ohio identified a one-third reduction in disorderly conduct—including 'loitering, panhandling, drinking, narcotics, gambling, and prostitution offenses'—in the business district over a seven-month period (Haberman & Stiver, 2019, p. 272). (See also the BID reports in the following chapter involving police and security patrols and reduced crime.)

In Queensland, an experiment in beat policing was conducted in the 1990s in Toowoomba in high-crime locations. The project included police officers living in their beat area (Criminal Justice Commission, 1995). Officers were meant to provide a highly visible presence and act proactively to solve local crime-related problems, especially those emanating from locations with repeat calls to police. The evaluation reported that residents were satisfied with the service but with no discernible increases in feelings of safety. During a time of rising crime, property crime rates remained stable in the experimental area while increasing in a comparison site.

Diverse Patrol Providers and Formats

Conventional public sector 'police' do not have a monopoly on preventive patrols, and a mix of public and private police is now a common form of visible 'policing'. Private security providers or 'parapolice' perform these same beat functions at publicly accessible private property locations such as shopping centres and entertainment venues, including making arrests using the powers available to them as the agents of property owners (Sarre & Prenzler, 2017). In addition, foot patrols in public spaces such as footpaths and parks can be conducted by security officers or both security officers and police in partnership. The security officers can be government employees, commercial in-house staff or the employees of contract security firms. Operatives' titles in these kinds of programs have included 'quality-of-life ambassadors', 'safety ambassadors', 'neighbourhood wardens', 'community wardens', 'street wardens', 'community support officers', 'municipal rangers' and 'peace workers' amongst others (Australian Institute of Health & Welfare, 2013, pp. 14–15; Cook & MacDonald, 2011, p. 499; Crawford et al., 2005, pp. 7 & 23; Piza et al., 2020, p. 657).

Parapolice can also be employees or volunteers within regular police forces, with variable powers. They can include cultural liaison officers, who interact with ethnic minority communities as well as more generalised 'community police' and also volunteers. England and Wales have seen significant developments in this domain. In 2023, for example, the Police Service listed 6,841 'special constables' and 7,806 'police community support officers' (PCSOs) alongside 147,430 police officers (Home Office, 2023, Table 2.1). Special constables are part-time volunteers with full police powers. PCSOs can issue on-the-spot fines for offences such as littering or riding a bike on a footpath, and they can confiscate alcohol and tobacco from young persons (Merrit & Dingwall, 2010). PCSOs do not carry weapons, but they have a limited detention authority if a person has engaged in anti-social behaviour or is a suspect in a crime and refuses to provide their name and address. The attraction of parapolice like these is that they cost less than fully sworn officers and have a focused set of skills and duties. They can specialise in face-to-face interactions with the public, assisting compliance, de-escalating conflict and calling fully sworn officers only when necessary.

Research by Merritt and Dingwall (2010) explored the views of PCSOs and their police managers operating in rural areas. There was a shared recognition that officers could assist victims of crime who would not normally reach out to police. Some support officers felt they could be empowered to deal with a wider range of crimes they encountered such as traffic offences. One manager reported that in the first year in which PCSOs were deployed, 'we cut anti-social behaviour and minor damage by about 40 per cent through being highly visible and going and talking to people all the time' (p. 394). In an article titled '"Soft" policing at hot spots—do police community support officers work? A randomized controlled trial', Ariel et al. (2016) found that the increased deployment of PCSOs on foot reduced crime by 39% compared to standard police vehicle patrols, with a 20% reduction in emergency calls for assistance.

Public–Private Partnerships

In terms of partnerships, a 2005 report, *Plural Policing: The Mixed Economy of Visible Patrols in England and Wales*, included accounts of five major collaborative policing programs that included private security officers in visible patrols in public areas (Crawford et al., 2005; see also Wakefield, 2003, chapter 6). The functions of these officers were described as follows (Crawford et al., 2005, p. 25):

- patrol function;
- crime prevention and problem-solving function;
- environmental management and improvement function;
- community engagement function;
- linking and referral function;
- information- and 'community intelligence'-gathering function and
- law enforcement function.

'Environmental management' included addressing 'the link between "grime and crime"' by notifying local authorities of maintenance issues, including those stemming from vandalism and graffiti (p. 28). A range of crime reduction effects were attributed to the work of these officers. For example (p. 25):

> In Bradford city centre where CSOs (community support officers) were first deployed, theft from a vehicle fell by 23% and theft of vehicle by 25%, while vehicle interference and tampering declined by 24%. Personal robbery declined by 46%. The greatest reductions occurred in crime 'hot-spot' areas, suggesting that patrol personnel were appropriately targeted through intelligence-led deployment. For many types of crime there does not appear to have been a significant displacement effect. However, some geographical displacement for certain types of crime, particularly theft from a vehicle, was apparent.

Other benefits included assisting in 'revitalising neighbourhoods and reconnecting people' (p. 28), and bridging 'institutional gaps' by linking people in need to appropriate service providers (p. 30).

As one example of a large-scale partnership, Crawford et al. (2005) described innovations in the enormous retail and leisure complex Metro-Centre in Northumbria in the United Kingdom. In 2002, centre management formed a partnership with local police in which it funded the employment of eight police officers as 'community beat managers' to staff a small police station, provide patrols, and work with centre management and retailers on crime prevention (p. 102). The partnership included employing a security firm, with 64 officers complementing the police. The security program also included a smaller in-house security team.

Public opinion surveys suggest that most people find the presence of security officers to be reassuring (Nalla et al., 2017; van Steden & Nalla, 2010). However, the nature of interactions mediates these views, as it does with police, leading to the conclusion that 'the industry needs to incorporate elements that heighten the security guards' image, as well as their utility to be an effective and trusted presence in quasi-public spaces where a large amount of public life takes part' (van Steden & Nalla, 2010, p. 219).

It should also be noted that foot patrols can operate in conjunction with police beat 'shopfronts'—mini police stations located in busy areas such as town centres and shopping centres, sometimes employing volunteers at the front desk (Piza et al., 2020; Taylor & Charlton, 2005). And, although 'foot' patrols are the focus of these types of patrol programs, they can include a range of wheeled vehicles other than cars, including segways and bicycles.

PUBLIC SPACE CCTV SYSTEMS

Public space CCTV systems have been a popular anti-crime measure in many locations. Optimal systems connect police and/or security officers on the streets with live monitoring personnel to ensure rapid responses to incidents. Evaluations of systems have shown very mixed results, with some successful case studies and others showing static or increased crime rates (Prenzler & Wilson, 2019). CCTV is an attractive option for citizen activists who are looking for a quick solution to public disorder problems and they will pressure politicians to instal or expand camera systems at taxpayers' expense. This often occurs without proper evaluation protocols in place and with no evidence of a crime reduction effect (Prenzler & Wilson, 2019).

Of note is a 2011 evaluation of camera programs in Baltimore, Chicago and Washington DC, which affirmed previous findings about factors that make for success in public space CCTV. The evaluation (La Vigne et al., 2011) found that, in downtown Baltimore, total crime in the camera areas was reduced by 24.8% four months after the installation of cameras. In Chicago, in the Humboldt Park area, all crime was reduced by 19.1% following installation of cameras. However, there were no notable changes in crime rates in the West Garfield Park area nor were there reductions in crime rates in Washington. The researchers identified the concentration of cameras and active monitoring as key factors in success. In the La Vigne et al. study, for Baltimore, it was estimated that, for every US$1 spent, US$1.06 was saved in costs associated with crime. For Chicago, the ratio was US$1:2.81. The study also emphasised the fact that community consultation was essential to ensure community support. CCTV can also provide wider benefits by alerting authorities to accidents and injuries, and people sleeping rough or in need of other forms of assistance.

ADDING WELFARE COMPONENTS TO PATROLS

The above discussion included a reference to a role for patrol officers in linking distressed persons to welfare services. As one example, police foot and vehicle patrols are sometimes augmented with access to mental health crisis teams. These 'first-responder police-mental health co-response teams' provide a wholistic means of managing mental health crises, whether occurring in private or public spaces (Bailey et al., 2018, p. 1). A key function of these teams is to de-escalate conflict, ensure safety for all stakeholders and bystanders, reduce police use-of-force including fatal shootings, and divert subjects away from the criminal justice system and into appropriate care. Bailey et al. (2018) examined experiences with 'mobile crisis assistance teams' (MCAT) in an Indianapolis pilot, which included paramedics along with police and mental health specialists. Focus groups and interviews showed that these groups could work well together but not without some friction. Key requirements for success included mutual respect, role clarification, adequate training, team building and access to suitable facilities.

'Street service care providers' are another category of welfare providers that can conduct patrols parallel to, and independent of, police or in a more coordinated format (Taylor et al., 2020, p. 21). These groups make themselves available in night-time entertainment locations to assist distressed or intoxicated persons. This type of service involves a variety of formats and names. They can include paid operators and/or volunteers and be resourced through government funding and/or donations. Workers generally engage in patrol to optimise their reach, and they can also operate out of premises that provide a contact point and safe haven for clients—such as 'chill out zones'. Other services include the provision of water, first aid and conflict reduction.

Adding a welfare, or wellbeing, component to patrols in hot spots for crime and disorder need not mean that police and security officers revert to a detached enforcement role and leave wider harm reduction interventions to other groups. A best practice model will involve a cultural shift amongst enforcement-oriented officers, with police and security providers actively prioritising harm reduction, including by working closely with welfare groups and initiating welfare-focused programs where needed. Deploying large numbers of female patrol officers is also likely to enhance the welfare and service aspects of patrol work (Schuck & Rabe-Hemp, 2024). It also needs to be emphasised that co-operative systems that include a strong referral or 'linking' function require bricks-and-mortar services in close proximity to where problems occur so that patrol services have somewhere to quickly take people who need help (Bailey et al., 2018; Crawford et al., 2005). Refuges, crisis accommodation, supported accommodation, mental health services, drug dependency services, and sobering-up centres all need to be available and readily accessible, adequately and securely resourced and open when needed. This means that central business districts, which attract a diverse population, need to provide these services alongside services focused on the interests of mainstream customers and workers.

Case Studies

The following section provides accounts of diverse patrol systems, with at least some evidence of a beneficial effect and with options for policy makers to consider. They include a networked CCTV system, Indigenous night patrols, a chaplaincy service in an entertainment precinct, and a multi-pronged community-based crime prevention program.

Networked CCTV in Newcastle upon Tyne

The Newcastle upon Tyne City Centre Partnership Security Initiative is one of the few open-space CCTV programs showing significant reductions in crime (Brown, 1995). The system was set up in 1992 with a combination of local private sector money and a government grant. Sixteen cameras were installed with zoom, pan and tilt capability. Police managed the system, with the CCTV control room linked by radio to patrol officers and retailers. Data about the concentration of crimes were used to locate cameras.

According to Brown (1995, p. 26), the system had a 'strong deterrent effect'. Cameras assisted rapid interventions by police, and the rate of arrests per criminal incident increased. The system also assisted with convictions: 'Almost all of the 400 people arrested as a direct result of the scheme admitted guilt after being shown video footage' (Brown, 1995, p. 26). The evaluation reported the average number of incidents across a range of crime types for 26 months before the program was fully implemented and compared these with the average number for 15 months following implementation. Key findings for the area within the CCTV system were as follows (Brown, 1995, p. 17):

- Burglary was reduced by 57% from 40 incidents per month to 17 per month,
- Theft from motor vehicles declined by 50% (18 to 9),
- Theft of motor vehicles declined by 47% (17 to 9),
- Criminal damage declined by 34% (32 to 21),
- Other theft declined by 11% (223 to 198).

While the rate of arrests increased relative to the number of recorded offences, the overall number of arrests decreased as offences decreased. In addition, a diffusion of benefits was observed in adjoining areas, which experienced substantial, albeit smaller, reductions in crimes.

Indigenous Night Patrols in Australia

'Community night patrols' have been implemented in numerous Indigenous communities in Australia beginning in the remote town of Tenant Creek in the late 1980s. A 2013 report identified 117 government-supported programs (Australian Institute of Health & Welfare, 2013, p. 7). The initiative involves volunteers and/or paid community members patrolling the streets of a community—usually at night and in a vehicle—offering support to those at risk of offending and/or victimisation. The patrols often focus on intoxicated persons, and they operate in part as a diversion from arrest and incarceration by taking potential arrestees home or to a 'sobering-up shelter'. Harm reduction is the principal aim. More broadly, the patrol groups can serve as an alternative means of justice and peacekeeping in mediating disputes, providing security at events and advising courts (Blagg & Valuri, 2004).

These patrols have become embedded in many communities. Despite the absence of strict scientific evaluations, the available evidence in support of diverse benefits has been summed up as follows (Australian Institute of Health & Welfare, 2013, p. 2):

- Monitoring data on community patrols in two remote communities in Western Australia suggests that they can substantially reduce the number of admissions to police lock-ups in some communities.
- Other reported outcomes from patrols include reduced juvenile crime rates when the patrols operated; reductions in alcohol-related harm and crime; improved partnerships and cultural understanding between Indigenous and non-Indigenous communities, and empowerment of the community...
- Patrols have associated benefits for communities, including employing local people and building community capacity to deal with community issues.

Survey research amongst community members also supports the positive impacts of patrols on feelings of safety at levels between 47 and 90% (p. 13). To be effective, patrols need to be seen to be independent of police while also working with them when required.

Cairns Street Chaplains
Taylor et al. (2020) conducted what is reputed to be the first systematic evaluation of this type of service in the form of Cairns Street Chaplains in Australia, initiated in 2013. The voluntary service is described as follows (Cairns Street Chaplains, 2023):

Cairns Street Chaplains provide a Good Samaritan service for alcohol or drug intoxicated and other vulnerable people in the Safe Night Precinct of Cairns every Friday and Saturday night. We are on the streets from 10.30pm to 4am offering both Rest and Recovery and Assertive Outreach support.

Our Rest and Recovery Point is at a van located on the corner of Grafton and Shields Streets. From here clients are rehydrated with cups of water, receive basic first aid, have a safe place to rest and chat for a while. They can recharge their phones or be referred on to other service providers, or into the care of a sober friend or family member.

Assertive Outreach is undertaken on foot as we patrol the streets in the Safe Night Precinct of Cairns actively looking for those in need of assistance, and offering basic first aid, help to get clients home safely by calling a sober friend or family member, walking clients to accommodation, taxis or buses, giving directions, having a chat and by referring on to other service providers including the Rest and Recovery Point.

We're part of a team in the city working with police, paramedics, taxi rank marshals, nightclub venue security, Cairns Regional Council employed security and the CitySafe CCTV Camera Room to keep the night club precinct of Cairns safe.

Volunteers receive specialist training and must hold first aid qualifications. The service is managed by the Cairns Christian Ministers Network and receives partial state government financial support. Approximately 300 persons receive assistance each week.

The program was introduced in the absence of other changes that might have affected incidents in the Cairns night-time entertainment area. The evaluation was focused on incidents occurring during 'high-alcohol hours', covering the period from January 2009 to January 2018. The study found that there was a significant reduction in police-recorded 'serious assaults' following the introduction of the service in 2013: averaging 1.6 less cases per month (Taylor et al., 2020, p. 26), although the causal mechanisms were not identified. Police-recorded 'common assaults' also showed a decline, although the difference pre- and post- was not statistically significant. No significant impacts were found for ambulance attendances or hospital emergency department presentations for injuries. Despite these mixed results, the researchers noted that anecdotal evidence also indicated that the service helped reduce harms associated with numerous (unspecified) incidents that would not normally come to the attention of police or ambulance services. (See also Moore, Sivarajasingam & Heikkinen's, 2013 evaluation of the Cardiff Alcohol Treatment Centre Pilot.)

The Adachi Ward Partnership

Hino and Chronopoulos (2021) reported on the 'Beautiful Windows Movement', introduced in 2008 in the Adachi Ward of Tokyo, based on broken windows, CPTED and reassurance policing principles. In the early

2000s, the Ward 'experienced the highest crime rates in central Tokyo and was perceived as a crime-ridden area' (p. 342). The initiative included a police focus on minor crimes, beautification and improvement of public spaces, a bicycle security program, citizen and private security patrols and resident access to a crime map. Six hundred and seventy cameras were installed, although it appeared that these only had accessible recordings without networked live monitoring. The citizen patrols—involving 'crime prevention volunteers'—included both foot and vehicle formats (p. 349). These had a strong focus on child protection, with a concentration on patrols at times when students walk to and from school. Volunteers were also involved in cleaning and planting flowers. The private security contract was awarded on a competitive basis, involving 24–7 patrols in 3–4 marked vehicles. Patrol routes were determined between the security company, ward office and police, with police briefings to patrol officers. Private security officers do not get involved in arrests but report incidents to police (Prenzler & Sarre, 2023, p. 79). According to Hino and Chronopoulos (2021), Adachi Ward experienced a 62.6% decline in crime from 2007 to 2019, the largest reduction amongst 23 wards in Tokyo. By 2013, a majority of residents surveyed described security as 'good'. Nonetheless, the authors noted that CCTV can be seen by citizens as a failure of social guardianship.

Conclusion

In order to feel safe, citizens want to see legitimate authorities in protective roles in public places and one of the best ways to do this is through visible uniformed patrols by police or different kinds of parapolice. The idea with preventive patrols is to minimise arrests and use-of-force, and rely instead as much as possible on deterrence, de-escalation, assistance and problem-solving to minimise crime and disorder (see the enforcement pyramid in Chapter 2). This is a good model but to fully develop its potential it needs to be augmented with the inclusion of more welfare-oriented specialists who can productively address issues of drug addiction, mental illness and homelessness.

References

Ariel, B., Weinborn, C., & Sherman, L. W. (2016). "Soft" policing at hot spots—Do police community support officers work? A randomized controlled trial.

Journal of Experimental Criminology, 12(3), 277–317. https://doi.org/10.1007/s11292-016-9260-4

Australian Institute of Health and Welfare. (2013). *The role of community patrols in improving safety in indigenous communities.* https://www.aihw.gov.au/getmedia/6709c52a-95f0-4592-a1b9-78a429638fb6/14455.pdf.aspx?inline=true

Bailey, K., Rising Paquet, S., Ray, B., Grommon, E., Lowder, E., & Sightes, E. (2018). Barriers and facilitators to implementing an urban co-responding police-mental health team. *Health and Justice, 6*(21), 1–12.

Blagg, H., & Valuri, G. (2004). Aboriginal community patrols in Australia: Self-policing, self-determination and security. *Policing & Society, 14*(4), 313–328.

Braga, A., Welsh, B., & Schnell, C. (2019). *Disorder policing to reduce crime: A systematic review.* Campbell Collaboration.

Brown, B. (1995). *CCTV in town centres: Three case studies.* Home Office.

Cairns Street Chaplains. (2023). cairnsstreetchaplains.org.au

Cook, P., & MacDonald, J. (2011). Public safety through private action: An Economic assessment of BIDS. *The Economic Journal, 121*(May), 445–462.

Crawford, A., Lister, S., Blackburn, S., & Burnett, J. (2005) *Plural policing: The Mixed economy of visible patrols in England and Wales.* Policy Press.

Criminal Justice Commission. (1995). *Toowoomba beat policing pilot project: Main evaluation report.* Author.

Drew, J. M., & Prenzler, T. (2015). *Contemporary police practice.* Oxford University Press.

Haberman, C., & Stiver, W. (2019). The Dayton foot Patrol program: An evaluation of hot spots foot patrols in a central business district. *Police Quarterly, 22*(3), 247–277.

Hino, K., & Chronopoulos, T. (2021). A review of crime prevention activities in a Japanese local government area since 2008: Beautiful windows movement in Adachi Ward. *Crime Prevention and Community Safety, 23*(1), 341–357.

Home Office. (2023). *Police workforce, England and Wales: 31 March 2023.* https://www.gov.uk/government/statistics/police-workforce-england-and-wales-31-march-2023/police-workforce-england-and-wales-31-march-2023

La Vigne, N., Lowry, S., Markman, J., & Dwyer, A. (2011). *Evaluating the use of public surveillance cameras for crime prevention.* Community Oriented Policing Service, US Department of Justice; and Justice Policy Center, Urban Institute.

Merritt, J., & Dingwall, G. (2010). Does plural suit rural? Reflections on quasi-policing in the countryside. *International Journal of Police Science & Management, 12*(3), 388–400. https://doi-org.ezproxy.usc.edu.au/10.1350/ijps.2010.12.3.178

Metcalfe, C., & Pickett, J. (2018). The extent and correlates of public support for deterrence reforms and hot spots policing. *Law and Society Review*, *52*(2), 471–502.

Moore, S., Sivarajasingam, V., & Heikkinen, M. (2013). *An evaluation of the Cardiff alcohol treatment Centre pilot*. Cardiff University Violence and Society Research Group.

MORI. (2005). *Summary of MORI findings for GLA*. https://www.ipsos.com/sites/default/files/migrations/en-uk/files/Assets/Docs/Archive/Polls/gla-dec.pdf

Nalla, M., Maxwell, S., & Mamayek, C. (2017). Legitimacy of private police in developed, emerging, and transitional economies. *Journal of Crime, Criminal Law and Criminal Justice*, *25*(1), 76–100.

Pate, A., Skogan, W., Wycoff, M., & Sherman, L. (1985). *Reducing the 'signs of crime': The Newark experience*. Police Foundation.

Piza, E., Wheeler, A., Connealy, N., & Feng, S. (2020). Crime control effects of a police substation within a business improvement district: A quasi-experimental synthetic control evaluation. *Criminology and Public Policy*, *19*(2), 653–684.

Prenzler, T., & Sarre, R. (2017). The security industry and crime prevention. In T. Prenzler (Ed.), *Understanding crime prevention: The case study approach* (pp. 167–183). Australian Academic Press.

Prenzler, T., & Sarre, R. (2023). Public space crime prevention partnerships: Reviewing the evidence. In E. Blackstone, S. Hakim, & B. Meehan (Eds.), *Handbook on public and private security* (pp. 67–84). Springer.

Prenzler, T., & Wilson, E. (2019). The Ipswich (Queensland) safe city program: An evaluation. *Security Journal*, *32*(2), 137–152.

Ratcliffe, J., Groff, E., Sorg, E., & Haberman, C. (2015). Citizens' reactions to hot spots policing: Impacts on perceptions of crime, disorder, safety and police. *Journal of Experimental Criminology*, *11*(3), 393–417.

Schuck, A., & Rabe-Hemp, C. (2024). Women police, legitimacy and the ethics of care. *Policing: A Journal of Policy and Practice*, *18*(1), 1–11.

Taylor, N., & Charlton, K. (2005). Police shopfronts and reporting to police by retailers. *Trends and Issues in Crime and Criminal Justice*, *205*, 1–6.

Taylor, N., Coomber, K., Curtis, A., Mayshaki, R., Harries, T., Ferris, J., Patafio, B., Hide, L., De Andrade, D., & Miller, P. (2020). The impact of street service care on frontline service utilisation during high-alcohol use hours in one night-time entertainment precinct in Australia. *Drug and Alcohol Review*, *39*(1), 21–28.

The Police Foundation. (2020). *Public safety and security in the 21st century*. https://www.policingreview.org.uk/wp-content/uploads/phase_1_report_final-1.pdf?mc_cid=d7d15e595c&mc_eid=5a36b24a10

The Police Foundation. (2022). *A new mode of protection: Redesigning policing and public safety for the 21st century.* https://www.policingreview.org.uk/wp-content/uploads/srpew_final_report.pdf

Trojanowicz, R. (1982). *Evaluation of the neighborhood foot patrol program in flint.* Michigan State University.

Trojanowicz, R., & Bucqueroux, B. (1990). *Community policing: A contemporary perspective.* Anderson.

van Steden, R., & Nalla, M. (2010). Citizen satisfaction with private security guards in the Netherlands. *European Journal of Criminology, 7*(3), 214–234.

Wakefield, A. (2003). *Selling security: The private policing of public space.* Willan Publishing.

Wakefield, A. (2006). *The value of foot patrol: A review of research.* The Police Foundation.

CHAPTER 4

Business Improvement Districts, Urban Regeneration and Social Inclusion

Abstract Business Improvement Districts (BIDs)—which include upgraded amenities and security—have been associated with reductions in crime and enhancements to business and shopping environments. Increasing attention is now being given to the welfare aspects of these types of programs, and this chapter elaborates on this trend, emphasising the need to integrate business facilitation with both safety and social inclusion. The chapter draws on numerous examples including BIDs in Figuero Corridor, Hollywood, Newark, Minneapolis, Washington DC, Winnipeg and Malmo. BIDs attest to the value of crime prevention partnerships and focused urban regeneration programs more generally, with large scope to include substantive crime prevention and welfare enhancement components.

Keywords Business improvement districts · Urban renewal · Diffusion of benefits · Social inclusion

BID Structures and Functions

Business Improvement Districts, or BIDs, are an area of public–private cooperation where there has been extensive innovation and numerous exemplar programs. Alternative terms include 'Business Improvement Associations' and 'Business Improvement Zones' (Walby & King, 2022, p. 226). BIDs involve systematic efforts to improve commerce by enhancing the amenity and civility of an area—usually town centres and similar open-air locations with street shops. Funds from governments and businesses are used to upgrade public areas by improving landscaping and seating, intensifying cleaning, removing graffiti, repairing vandalised property, removing abandoned vehicles, sealing empty buildings to prevent squatting, upgrading lighting and introducing or enlarging police or security patrols (Hoyt, 2004; Moir et al., 2024). The core idea, consistent with CPTED theory, is to attract legitimate users, improve guardianship and deter offenders. Visible uniformed security patrols of the type discussed in the preceding chapter are a common feature.

BIDs have been traced back to the late 1960s in North America, with one estimate putting the number in the United States in the early 2000s at approximately 2,000 (Jones et al., 2003, p. 51). Brockie (2019) reported there were 305 BIDs in the British Isles in 2018 (p. 8). Los Angeles has seen the creation of numerous BIDs. These are generally approved and regulated by local government, and 'managed and operated by private non-profit organisations' (Cook & MacDonald, 2011, p. 448). Levies are often compulsorily obtained from all property owners and/or businesses within a BID. However, extensive consultation occurs before BIDs are established, and significant support must be expressed through signed petitions. In the Los Angeles case, the city government has provided financial assistance for planning purposes. BIDs in the city tend to be focused on sanitation and crime: '"Clean" and "safe" are common terms used by BIDs in LA' (p. 448). Cook and MacDonald (2011) reported in their study that 'eleven of the 30 BIDs operating in LA in 2005 spent more than $200,000 a year on private security operations, with nearly equal amounts being spent on sanitation services' (2011, p. 448). Security officers generally eschew the use of citizen arrest powers or the powers of agents of property owners. Instead, they primarily work through personal contact, communication about rules and consequences, and offers of assistance. Although security officer calls for police backup appear to be rare, the ability to call police via radio appears as an important source of authority (D'Souza, 2020, p. 80).

BIDs, and similar partnership-based urban regeneration programs, represent a response 'to gaps in safety and security' (Walby & King, 2022, p. 225). As such, they represent a failure of democratic governance and also individualised security. At the same time, their presence, and moves to create new programs, represent a crucial opportunity for democratic governments to be responsive to citizen initiatives and wishes, and work with them to optimise a multi-faceted approach to urban revitalisation.

The Figueroa Corridor and Hollywood BIDs

Cook and MacDonald (2011) provided some detail on the Figueroa Corridor BID in Downtown Los Angeles and the Hollywood Entertainment BID (p. 499):

> The Figueroa Corridor BID was formed in 1998 by business property owners in direct response to economic decline and a concern with area crime. From the outset its efforts were focused on improving community safety by employing uniformed private security workers (Safety Ambassadors) who patrol the district on foot, bike and evening vehicle patrols and assist in keeping order. It spends close to $500,000 a year, or almost half of its operational budget, on these officers. This BID also employs cleaning crews that remove trash, debris and graffiti.
>
> The Hollywood Entertainment BID employs armed private security officers who are retired law enforcement officers. These officers patrol the Hollywood district seven days a week during evening hours, initiate citizen arrests when they observe violations of the law and work closely with the Los Angeles Police Department (LAPD). It spends just over $1 million a year on private security, or approximately 47% of its operating budget. It has also installed eight CCTV cameras at intersections in the district for use by the LAPD.

The Newark Downtown District

BIDs can include a variety of other features. A BID in Newark included a police substation, which served as a base for intensified foot and vehicle patrols (Piza et al., 2020). As part of the partnership agreement, BID funds were used to renovate and furnish the premises and pay rent, while police provided personnel. The Newark BID includes uniformed 'quality-of-life ambassadors' involved in diverse frontline order maintenance services, described as follows (Piza et al., 2020, p. 657):

> Perhaps the most visible component of the NDD's (Newark Downtown District) revitalization efforts are quality-of-life (QOL) ambassadors who travel throughout the downtown area (not just the substation target area) on foot for the purpose of identifying and rectifying problems that may impact the community. When they observe crime or disorder, QOL ambassadors report the incident via the two-way radio to request a police response... QOL ambassador reports predominantly relate to social (e.g., public intoxication, aggressive panhandling, etc.) and physical (e.g., illegal dumping, vandalization, etc.) disorder.

The Minneapolis Downtown Improvement District

Walby and King (2022) provided a description of the Minneapolis Downtown Improvement District (DID) established in 2005 'to stabilize the downtown environment in which businesses operate, residents live in, and tourists visit' (p. 228). At the time, 'Minneapolis was well known for homelessness, mental illness, and panhandling' (p. 229). All commercial entities are required to pay a levy, while charities, residences and government facilities are exempt. The program covers 120 city blocks. Governance is centred on a Board of Directors, 'composed of representatives from each of the downtown constituents' (p. 230). Staffing issues are largely managed by a 'Block by Block company'. Cleanliness and amenity are key areas of work. 'DID ambassadors' engage in frontline service provision, including the following (p. 230):

> hospitality and safety services (e.g. providing directions to others), cleaning (e.g. washing streets, litter collection), outreach (e.g. reporting and information sharing via electronic channel), landscaping, and grounds maintenance. Ambassadors may travel on foot, bicycle, or vehicles.

Improved safety was the primary concern of the DID initiative, organised around 'the Minneapolis SafeZone Collaborative' (Walby & King, 2022, p. 229). This involved the establishment of a live monitored camera system linked to police, security officers on private property and DID ambassadors. Other safety components include the Downtown Safety Partners and Strategic Justice Partnership involving guidance and shared intelligence from policing and criminal justice entities. One area of focus is the targeting of chronic repeat offenders, ostensibly based on support with arrest as a final resort option.

BID-Malmo

BID-Malmo in Sweden involves another set of features worth reviewing. It was established in 2014 to address problems of crime and disorder, including in areas suffering disadvantage. It has around 40 members, consisting of 'public and private property owners, housing cooperatives and local businesses' (Kronkvist & Ivert, 2020, p. 138). It was established without any special legislation. Membership is voluntary. Members work closely in a 'public–private partnership' with local police and local government (p. 138). Membership fees have supported a wide range of activities. Monies have (p. 139),

> financed additional cleaning of public environments, introduced a contract for joint graffiti removal among members, implemented community gardening initiatives and conducted visual environmental audits that have led to improvements to visually unpleasant and unsafe locations. BID-Malmö has also had a strong focus on making properties more secure via situational measures … This has in part been realised through security inspections of properties in collaboration with a local insurance company, which has resulted in installation of security doors and fortified locks in property entrances, increased lighting, etc. Members undergoing a security inspection and realising any potential flaws in security are offered a reduced insurance premium. In addition, the organisation has lobbied for, and succeeded in obtaining, police monitored camera surveillance along streets with high crime levels. In collaboration with the city's municipal offices, BID-Malmö has also restricted vehicular traffic along certain roads with the approval of the city's municipal offices.

IMPACTS

Evaluations of BIDs have shown variable results but a number of successes in reducing crime without displacement effects. One review stated that 'based on available statistics, most neighbourhoods with established BID security programs have experienced double-digit reductions in crime rates (sometimes up to 60 per cent) in the years following their creation'

(Vindevogel, 2005, p. 237). Police backup is considered essential to the success of security operations in BIDs (p. 249). A 2009 evaluation also noted additional requirements for wider success (MacDonald et al., 2009, p. xv):

> BIDs that are active and have enough capital to hire private security, clean streets of trash and debris, and organize with city service agencies to address merchant or property owner concerns about community needs are more effective agents of community-level change.

Walby and King (2022) reported on a program within the Minneapolis DID that applied an enforcement pyramid to repeat offenders, reportedly resulting in 'a 74% reduction in downtown Minneapolis crime by "chronic offenders" on the DID's 100 list compared to the previous year' (p. 230).

BIDs also tend to make police more accountable by focusing on business owners' expectations of a police response and by channelling calls for assistance through one phone link. At the same time, the evidence appears to support the idea that BIDs will ultimately reduce calls to police and demands on police time. The process, along with associated benefits, is described by Vindevogel (2005, p. 250):

> Even if police officers in the field do have to respond to the solicitations of the BIDs and react to such problems as disorderly youths or street peddling, there is no doubt that BID security officers take appropriate measures more often. They not only take on a whole array of responsibilities that police officers have to assume in the absence of other easily identifiable 'guardians' (they give directions, help find lost property, assist lost children, etc.) but they also take charge of all these quality-of-life violations that police officers traditionally dislike handling because, as they argue, it diverts them from 'real police work'. More importantly, thanks to their deterrent visibility and communication skills these security officers also anticipate problems and prevent tensions from escalating: they stop disputes before they degenerate into fights, create safety corridors between high schools and subway stations, etc. Finally, BIDs centralize requests: when local retailers or corporate security directors have safety-related concerns, they frequently solicit BID instead of calling 911 or their precinct.

This can all be done without the security officers taking on any powers beyond those of ordinary citizens (Vindevogel, 2005).

More recently, Moir et al. (2024) conducted the first systematic assessment of BID impacts on crime and disorder. The researchers reviewed 13 published evaluations. The large majority—11/13—were conducted in the United States, with three in Los Angeles and three in Philadelphia. There was one evaluation from Canada and one from Sweden. Nine studies included quantitative measures of crime and/or disorder, with pre- and post-intervention data and comparison sites. The main summary findings were as follows (p. 4):

> Of the nine studies that quantitatively examined BID impacts on crime rates, eight (88%) found a reduction in one or more crime types. Six studies explored BID impacts on property crime, with all finding BIDs had a significant negative association with at least one type of property crime, with BIDs particularly effective at targeting vehicle related offences. BIDs were also found to have a positive impact on reducing disorder and public nuisance type offences, however, had mixed evidence on violent crime, with three out of seven studies on violent crime finding BIDs can help to prevent robbery.

Violence

The findings from the Moir et al. (2024) study were, therefore, very mixed, but tending towards a case in favour of the potential for BIDs to improve safety and security. The area of violent crime was perhaps most disappointing, given that reductions in violence provide a key aim and rationale for BIDs. One should expect large reductions in assaults, for example. As noted, robbery was the only category of violence showing reductions—in three studies—while one study found there had been a significant rise in street robberies and four studies showing no significant changes. Possible explanations for this include the idea that any reductions in violent crime are offset by the fact that BIDs attract more potential offenders and more potential victims (Clutter et al., 2019; Moir et al., 2024). It has also been argued that many violent crimes like robberies also tend to be more hidden (Hoyt, 2005).

Property Crime

Six of the evaluations in the Moir et al. (2024) review included property crime impacts and all six studies found declines in at least one category. For example (p. 10):

> Hoyt (2004) found that property crime in both BID and non-BID areas declined in Philadelphia from 1998-2001, with property crimes in BIDs declining at a rate more than double that of non-BIDs (5% in BIDs vs 2.3% in non-BDs). They found similar results in a later study where property crimes (including theft, theft from and of vehicles) were lower in commercial areas with BIDs compared to areas without BIDs in Philadelphia across a four-year period (Hoyt, 2005). In a later study of a police substation in a Philadelphia BID, significant reductions in burglary and motor-vehicle theft were identified (Piza et al., 2020). Across the three-year period following implementation, the BID experienced roughly 72 and 56 fewer motor-vehicle thefts and burglaries, respectively, but also recorded roughly 86 more theft from auto vehicles offences during this period. Long term (three-to-six years post implementation), significant reductions were found for both theft from auto vehicles (70 fewer offences) and theft from motor-vehicles (66 fewer offences), while no significant differences were found for burglary.

Outside the United States, the Swedish case study from Malmo included quantitative impact measures. Significant declines were recorded for burglary (-39.6%, compared to -29.2% in the control) and vandalism (-6.5%, compared to $+ 23.9\%$ in the control) (Kronkvist & Ivert, 2020, p. 146).

In terms of explanations for reductions in property crime, Hoyt (2004) associated reductions in crimes such as theft and burglary with the deterrent effect of uniformed security officers, while Piza et al. associated reductions in motor vehicle thefts and parking violations with a more proactive policing style, especially targeted visible police patrols and (unspecified) '"quality-of-life" summonses' (2020, p. 655). In the case of the Malmo BID, Kronkvist and Ivert (2020, p. 147) argued that:

> The observed reduction in property crimes is in line with what might be expected based on the measures taken by BID-Malmö to secure properties by means of different situational crime prevention techniques such as the installation of safety doors and fortified locks on property entrances. In addition, improvements in the physical environment, enhanced public

area maintenance and improved security may also have contributed to the decline via increased informal and formal social control in the intervention neighbourhood, which may have deterred potentially motivated burglars.

Disorder

The systematic review of BID impact evaluations by Moir et al. (2024) included three studies with quantitative data on the disorder and associated anti-social behaviours. Two of these identified significant reductions in this area (Han et al., 2017; Kronkvist & Ivert, 2020). The third study, by Hoyt (2005) in Philadelphia, found no major differences in the category of disorderly conduct between BID and non-BID locations. However, also in Philadelphia, Han et al. (2017) identified significant reductions in 'nuisance crimes of graffiti, illegal dumping, and disorderly conduct' in 15 BIDs over a five-year period (pp. 667–668). In the Malmo BID, Kronkvist and Ivert (2020) found reductions in vandalism post-implementation compared to a control location.

Moir et al. (2024) also located four qualitative studies of BID impacts in the area of disorder. Based on interviews with BID leaders and staff in Washington DC, Lee and Ferguson (2019) concluded that outreach and support services helped reduce homelessness and assisted unemployed persons to find work (see more below). Walby and King (2022) provided largely descriptive accounts of the Minneapolis Downtown Improvement District and Winnipeg Downtown Community Safety Partnership, indicating some possible reductions in disorder but primarily from exclusions rather than welfare (see also Howe, 2023 and Kudla, 2022). Vindevogel (2005) used diverse sources, including official statistics and interviews, to assess BIDs in Philadelphia and New York City. The author was positive in regard to their effects. Specifically, the Times Square BID was considered successful in reducing the number of sex shops and an associated sleazy atmosphere, attracting more family-based entertainment. The work of security officers was associated with reducing disputes, 'quiet(ing) down disorderly groups', and dispelling pickpockets and scam gambling game operators (p. 244).

D'Souza (2020) used interviews and observations to examine the impacts of the work of Public Safety Officers (PSOs) engaged in street patrols in four BIDs. She found that the officers made contributions to the quality-of-life in the BIDs, mainly through encouraging homeless persons to move on, referring to cleaning and maintenance issues (including follow-up checks), sharing information on drug dealing with police and discouraging illegal street vendors. The officers used politeness and rapport—key elements of procedural justice (Chapter 2)—as compliance and personal safety strategies. The following example illustrates the application of this soft power approach to compliance (p. 80):

> Many panhandlers stood in front of near business entrances or in the middle of the sidewalk. Although most moved with little to no pushback, during one interaction, a man with a large sign requesting change refused to move from a store entrance citing his "First Amendment rights." In response, the PSO silently stood beside him; this largely deterred pedestrians from giving him money, forcing the panhandler to leave the area. PSOs frequently discussed how, due to their lack of traditional enforcement, they had to rely on other seemingly more creative strategies to garner the public's compliance.

Displacement and Diffusion of Benefits

Moir et al. (2024) also located four studies which examined displacement effects. Three of the four found there was no evidence of any substantial displacement. These included Hoyt (2005) and Cook and MacDonald (2011). The latter also identified a modest but significant reduction in arrests for auto theft offences in adjacent locations. The Malmo study by Kronkvist and Ivert (2020) also found a likely diffusion of benefits. All crime declined by 13.0% in the BID and by 10.4% in the immediate surrounding area (p. 146). In their study of a BID in Philadelphia, Piza et al. (2020) identified a diffusion of benefits for burglary and motor vehicle theft but likely displacement of robbery and theft from vehicles to surrounding areas. It has been argued that displacement is unlikely as many of the types of crime occurring in BIDs do not translate easily to adjoining residential areas and policing patrols might venture into surrounding peripheries (Cook & MacDonald, 2011; Hoyt, 2005; Moir et al., 2024, pp. 15–16).

Financial Cost–Benefit Assessments

Economic assessments of BIDs have found they can provide significant public value, apart from reducing victimisation. By reducing crime, they also reduce the costs of criminal justice processing of arrested offenders (Cook & MacDonald, 2011; see also Welsh et al., 2015). Moir et al. (2024) identified three cost—benefit assessments of BIDs, 'with all finding BIDs to be value for money' (p. 14), summarised as follows:

Cook and MacDonald's (2011) study found that 28 fewer serious crimes in each BID translated into savings of between (US)$183,000 and $208,000, compared to BID costs of $10,000. Adding arrest savings of $5,000 produced a cost-benefit ratio between (US)$18.8 and $21.3 for every dollar spent. Welsh et al.'s (2015) review of the cost-benefits of criminal justice programs found that while benefits exceed costs for most crime prevention programs, this was especially so for target hardening, improved lighting, and BID programs. Welsh et al. (2015) considered Cook and MacDonald's (2011) findings as evidence of BIDs being the most cost-beneficial community programs available, alongside community development programs. Brooks' (2008) large, longitudinal study of crime and arrest impacts found that BIDs in Los Angeles on average spent (US)$150,000 per annum, with $50,000 spent on security services. They found that BIDs spent $21,000 to prevent one violent crime, which was substantially lower than the $57,000 conservative social cost of a violent crime, leading to the conclusion that 'BIDs are cheap' (p. 401).

Better Business and an Improved Environment

One oddity of the BID evaluation literature is the preoccupation with a crime in the absence of both quantitative and qualitative assessments of changes to business, numbers of shoppers and visitors and general amenities. Data on feelings of safety are also missing. BIDs have been credited with 'restoring urban morale and making older downtowns more attractive places to shop, visit, do business, and seek entertainment' (Briffault, 1999, p. 370). However, statements of this kind do not tend to be well-attested. Improvements tend to be assumed rather than documented. Briffault refers to a report on New York City BIDs by MacDonald (1996), which cites two law firms who moved to the Grand Central Partnership BID in support of the 'economic argument' for BIDs, as well as 'zero vacancy rates of many buildings' in the vicinity of the Bryant Park BID. According to MacDonald (1996), the Bryant Park area,

> had become a glaring symbol of the city's inability to control its public spaces. The park was a haven for drug dealers and petty criminals; shootouts and assaults were common. Law-abiding workers in the area feared and shunned the park, and surrounding property values had taken a nosedive.

Following the establishment of the BID,

> Overnight, the park became the most successful public square in the city, showered with awards. Round-the-clock security and an exacting standard of maintenance keep the space safe and immaculate—even down to its public toilets. The crowds thronging the park throughout the day and evening have belied the charge that it would become the exclusive province of the rich. 'I have yet to see turnstiles,' muses Lieb [a property owner]. 'No one has ever said: "You can't go into the park." They have said: "You can't urinate on the bushes and attack people."' Property values around the park have risen; many buildings have waiting lists for tenants. Former critics of the Bryant Park BID are now unabashed supporters.

Overall, however, the wider set of arguments for BIDs is an area that requires systematic evaluation.

Funding Sources and BID-Style Programs

Member levies are commonly included in descriptions of BIDs. It appears that levies are often imposed on all businesses within a BID once a consultation and voting process results in a development being established. Charities, residences and government offices are usually exempt (Walby & King, 2022, p. 229). However, it is not clear from the literature whether or not levies and universal membership are essential characteristics of BIDs. And while BIDs appear to be cost-effective (above) some members might feel that they do not experience direct financial benefits. Others might feel that the adverse financial circumstances that might motivate BID development mean it is difficult for them to meet this additional cost impost. However, regardless of this definitional issue, it does appear that 'BID-like' programs can be initiated without compulsory membership being included, such as the case with BID-Malmo (Kronkvist &

Ivert, 2020, p. 138). In addition, funds for developments can be sought from a variety of sources, including government investments, especially local government, and private donors. In theory, BID-style initiatives can operate on goodwill and formal agreements in which members commit to making specific changes voluntarily. Examples include business owners agreeing to in-house security measures; police agreeing to increase foot patrols; and councils agreeing to improve cleaning and maintenance. Governments and insurance companies can also provide tax and insurance discounts for businesses that upgrade security or engage in other enhancements (Kronkvist & Ivert, 2020).

This approach is likely to be especially important in impoverished locations, where local governments are cash-strapped and highly constrained in expanding their tax base and where insufficient businesses are willing to agree to mandated levies. Chapter 1 of this book identified a shortage of public funds as a major source of inadequate government protection services in public places. Courageous democratic governments need to tax the rich while ensuring they are also running a highly efficient operation free of waste and corruption and channel more public funds into improved security and amenity in shared spaces.

'BID-style' programs can be developed under various rubrics including 'safer cities', 'crime prevention councils' and associated 'urban regeneration' or 'downtown revitalisation' programs (Moir et al., 2024, p. 7; Piza et al., 2020, p. 657). A good example of this in a specific area involves the idea of local governments taking a lead in dealing with the problem of vacant premises. For example, the Local Government Association (2020) in the United Kingdom has published a guide *Dealing with empty shops—A good practice guide for councils*. Strategies include leveraging council monies and/or external grants to provide loans and grants for community groups and start-ups to take on tenancies. Heritage funding can also be used to renovate premises and rezoning can create more options—including for residential use.

Social Inclusion and Welfare

The discussion so far has highlighted the many potential benefits of BIDs in reducing crime and disorder and making business areas more attractive, vibrant and profitable. Nonetheless, BID or BID-style, programs have also been criticised as potentially elitist, undemocratic, involving a creeping privatisation of public security, placing profits above people and seeking to exclude marginalised groups considered undesirable (D'Souza, 2020; Howe, 2023; Walby & King, 2022). The latter can include young people, the unemployed, homeless persons and drug-dependent and mentally ill persons, some of whom can act in anti-social ways and cause fear by loitering. As we saw in Chapter 1, public spaces, such as commercial hubs and town centres, where BIDs are often implemented, are attractive to marginalised groups as safer locations where they can find a company and also engage in begging and street peddling. A snowball effect can occur in which charities and government services are located where marginalised persons congregate, thereby attracting more clients. This can incur a community backlash, with calls for relocation of services and/or better place management and protections (Prenzler et al., 2022, chapter 4).

From that perspective, BIDs and social inclusion might seem anti-thetical. However, there are some studies which suggest that social inclusion and welfare support policies can be part of productive BID-style programs. A social contract framework (Chapter 2) means that services can be provided while intimidating and predatory behaviour is not toler-ated. A 'liberal' perspective sometimes entails tolerance of people sleeping rough and engaging in anti-social conduct. However, there are major problems with this approach. These include the exposure of vulnerable persons on the streets to a range of harms, including assault, sexual assault and robbery. There are also major hygiene issues; general urban decline; genuine issues of public insecurity and the creation of 'no-go zones' (Police Foundation, 2020, p. 54; Prenzler et al., 2022, chapter 4). Chapter 3 discussed the need for on-site facilities to address the needs of marginalised persons. At the same time, in some cases, responsible management will involve placing some persons in secure facilities.

Case Studies

D'Souza's (2020) study of four BIDs in the United States found that homelessness was the primary challenge for BID staff. In three of the four BIDs, staff 'worked very closely with local shelters and outreach programs' (p. 78). Many of the security officers reported that they sought to link homeless persons with services, although most declined assis-tance and simply moved on. Frontline patrol officers in BIDs can provide useful information to authorities about the scale of the need for social support services: 'city officials might want to utilize the reports collected by PSOs (Public Safety Officers) on issues of homelessness and panhandlers, helping to improve their own social services and better aid these groups' (D'Souza, 2020, p. 82).

In another example of efforts to address welfare issues, Walby and King (2022) describe a service-oriented component of the Downtown Community Safety Partnership (DCSP) in Winnipeg (p. 233):

One aspect of the DCSP that is very different than what public police, private security, or BIA (Business Improvement Association) ambassadors provide is the attempt to offer some sort of services and supports to people in distress downtown. The Medical Assist and Connect (MAC247) and Community Outreach Advocacy Resource (COAR) teams are pillars of Winnipeg's DCSP... MAC247 deals with community and outreach services which includes social needs assessment, advanced first aide, and non-emergency medical situations. COAR provides wrap-around services, such as addictions treatment, education, mental health support, and other long-term supports to the community... The DCSP ... works with local First Nations and Métis leaders on these issues of addictions treatment, education, mental health support, and provision.

According to Walby and King (2022), DCSP staff are chosen for their skills in communication. They are considered much less aggressive than the police. BIZ (Business Improvement Zone) ambassadors 'engage in benevolent behaviour such as distributing food, water, and health care material to the distressed and unhoused people who they encounter in Winnipeg streets downtown' (p. 234). Nonetheless, the authors noted that the removal of persons deemed undesirable remains a key strategy.

Based on interviews with leaders and staff in three BIDs in Washington DC, Lee and Ferguson (2019) concluded that business members of BIDs often make major voluntary contributions to the welfare of disadvantaged persons in their BID area—in part through their own direct contributions and in part through the structure and functions of the BID. Assistance with finding housing and employment are the two primary examples. The Downtown DC BID includes a Homeless Outreach Service Team (HOST). According to Lee and Ferguson (2019), programs like these 'have helped many chronically homeless persons to move into permanent housing' (p. 393). The Capitol Hill BID operates a program Ready, Willing and Working (RWW), which links homeless persons and released prisoners to employment. The Executive Director reported that 'RWW has provided not only employment opportunities with a full benefits package and supportive services but also positive environments in which the employees transform their mindset and view of themselves' (p. 394).

CONCLUSION

Business Improvement Districts provide a valuable model for fixing overlapping problems of urban blight, business decline and crime in town centres and commercial hubs. There is good evidence to show that BIDs can improve public safety through the application of CPTED and situational prevention techniques. At the same time, the evidence regarding impacts on crime and disorder is sufficiently mixed to suggest that more needs to be done in existing BIDs to create safe spaces and that crime needs a much greater focus in BID planning (Brockie, 2019). BIDs can also develop services that address the needs of marginalised groups, although this is also an area where it is likely that much more can be done to improve social inclusion in BID-style programs.

REFERENCES

Briffault, R. (1999). Government for our time-business improvement districts and urban governance. *Columbia Law Review, 99*(2), 365–477.

Brockie, G. (2019). *Business improvement districts' contribution to crime reduction and the challenges they face in addressing levy payers' safety and security concerns.* https://nbcc.police.uk/images/news/The_BID_Safe__Secure_Rep ort.pdf

Brooks, L. (2008). Volunteering to be taxed: Business improvement districts and the extra-governmental provision of public safety. *Journal of Public Economics, 9*(2), 388–406.

Clutter, J., Henderson, S., & Haberman, C. (2019). The impact of business improvement district proximity on street block robbery counts. *Crime and Delinquency, 65*(8), 1050–1075.

Cook, P., & MacDonald, J. (2011). Public safety through private action: An economic assessment of BIDS. *The Economic Journal, 121*(May), 445–462.

D'Souza, A. (2020). An examination of order maintenance policing by business improvement districts. *Journal of Contemporary Criminal Justice, 36*(1), 70–85.

Han, S., Morçöl, G., Hummer, D., & Peterson, S. (2017). The effects of business improvement districts in reducing nuisance crimes: Evidence from Philadelphia. *Journal of Urban Affairs, 39*(5), 658–674.

Howe, A. (2023). The city and the city: Tent camps and luxury development in the NoMA Business Improvement District (BID) in Washington, D.C. *International Journal of Historical Archaeology, 28*(1), 165–181. https://doi.org/10.1007/s10761-022-00691-2

Hoyt, L. (2004). Collecting private funds for safe public spaces: An empirical examination of the business improvement district concept. *Environment & Planning b: Planning & Design, 31*(3), 367–380.

Hoyt, L. (2005). Do business improvement district organizations make a difference? Crime in and around commercial areas in Philadelphia. *Journal of Planning Education and Research, 25*(2), 185–199.

Jones, P., Hillier, D., & Comfort, D. (2003). Business improvement districts in town and city centres in the UK. *Management Research News, 26*(8), 50–58.

Kronkvist, K., & Ivert, A. (2020). A winning BID? The effects of a BID-inspired property owner collaboration on neighbourhood crime rates in Malmö, Sweden. *Crime Prevention and Community Safety, 22*(2), 134–152.

Kudla, D. (2022). Fifty years of business improvement districts: A reappraisal of the dominant perspectives and debates. *Urban Studies, 59*(14), 2837–2856.

Lee, W., & Ferguson, K. (2019). The role of local businesses in addressing multidimensional needs of homeless populations. *Journal of Human Behavior in the Social Environment, 29*(3), 389–402.

Local Government Association (UK). (2020). *Dealing with empty shops—A good practice guide for councils*. https://www.local.gov.uk/dealing-empty-shops-guide

MacDonald, H. (1996). BIDs really work. *The City Journal, 6*(Spring). https://www.city-journal.org/article/bids-really-work

MacDonald, J., Bluthenthal, R., Golinelli, D., Kofner, A., Stokes, R., Sehgal, A., & Fain, T. (2009). *Neighborhood effects on crime and youth violence. The role of Business Improvement Districts in Los Angeles*. RAND Corporation.

Moir, E., Cairns, N., Prenzler, T., & Rayment-McHugh, S. (2024). *A review of the impacts of Business Improvement Districts on crime and disorder.* Unpublished paper.

Piza, E., Wheeler, A., Connealy, N., & Feng, S. (2020). Crime control effects of a police substation within a business improvement district: A quasi-experimental synthetic control evaluation. *Criminology and Public Policy, 19*(2), 653–684.

Prenzler, T., Cairns, N., Moir, E., & Rayment-McHugh, S. (2022). *Nambour community safety review: Stage 1 report*. Sunshine Coast Council and University of the Sunshine Coast. https://research.usc.edu.au/esploro/outputs/report/Nambour-Community-Safety-Review-Stage-1/99680498102621?institution=61USC_INST#file-0

The Police Foundation. (2020). *Public safety and security in the 21st century*. https://www.policingreview.org.uk/wp-content/uploads/phase_1_report_final-1.pdf?mc_cid=d7d15e595c&mc_eid=5a36b24a10

Vindevogel, F. (2005). Private security and urban crime mitigation: A bid for BIDs. *Criminal Justice, 5*(3), 233–255.

Walby, K., & King, B. (2022). Community safety or corporate capture? Hybrid privatization of social control in a downtown core. *Crime Prevention and Community Safety, 24*(3), 224–238.

Welsh, B., Farrington, D., & Gowar, B. (2015). Benefit-cost analysis of crime prevention programs. *Crime and Justice, 44*(1), 447–516.

CHAPTER 5

Safe Orderly Efficient Transport Systems

Abstract Transport systems, including transport hubs, attract a wide range of predatory behaviours. Train and bus systems are prone to customer insecurity and dissatisfaction. This chapter examines best practice strategies that integrate safety with convenience, timeliness and cleanliness within a continuous improvement framework. In this topic area, it appears that a large array of situational interventions is essential. Enhanced human guardianship will inevitably be a centrepiece. The chapter includes a diverse set of case studies to highlight processes and interventions most likely to succeed, including limiting access, security patrols, networked CCTV and rapid graffiti removal.

Keywords Road safety · Graffiti · Motor vehicle theft · Patrols

Mechanised Transport Systems: A Pandora's Box of Problems

The development of mass public transport via trains and buses in the nineteenth and early twentieth centuries facilitated the growth of the 'divergent metropolis', with long commutes for workers and shoppers between home, workplaces and places of recreation (Felson & Eckert,

© The Author(s), under exclusive license to Springer Nature
Switzerland AG 2024
T. Prenzler, *Preventing Crime and Disorder in Public Places*, Crime
Prevention and Security Management,
https://doi.org/10.1007/978-3-031-63764-3_5

2018, p. 56). People were crowded together on platforms and in carriages in a crime smorgasbord. Travellers were subject to almost every form of affront imaginable including pickpocketing, bag snatching, harassment, robbery, assault, sexual assault and murder. Operators were subject to fare evasion and had to deal with often chronic rates of graffiti and vandalism. Passenger planes and airports became major targets for terrorist attacks from the 1970s—although security screening and intelligence-based pre-emption have greatly reduced this area of risk in the last two decades (Prenzler, 2018).

Some relief from the incivilities of public transport occurred in the latter part of the twentieth century when private cars became widely available and commuters could hide from the crowd in a bubble of steel and glass. However, this change brought its own set of problems, including pandemic-level crashes resulting in enormous numbers of deaths and horrific, often permanent, injuries. The most recent global data from the World Health Organisation (2023) on global road trauma are truly distressing (p. 3):

- There were an estimated 1.19 million road traffic deaths in 2021;
- As of 2019, road traffic injury remains the leading cause of death for children and young people aged 5–29 years and is the 12th leading cause of death when all ages are considered …;
- pedestrians … make up 23% of fatalities …;
- Cyclists account for 6% of fatalities;
- 3% of deaths are amongst users of micro-mobility devices such as e-scooters;
- 92% of deaths occur in low- and middle-income countries.

Vehicle crashes and associated harms stem from a mix of causes including driver inattention, distraction, fatigue, risk-taking, speeding, drug and alcohol impairment, and lack of seat belt use (Bates et al., 2016; World Health Organization, 2023). Road and vehicle design also play a major part, including factors such as poor visibility and lack of barriers on roads. Underenforcement of safety laws is also a major contributor, reducing the deterrent and incapacitation effects of detection and sanctioning, especially in regard to the behaviour of repeat high-risk offenders (Prenzler & Sarre, 2021, pp. 292–293).

The spread of motorised vehicles contributed to a wide range of other crime and disorder problems. Vehicle thefts and thefts from vehicles became major volume crimes in developed countries from the 1970s, and motor vehicles facilitated offender access to targets and quick escapes with a convenient means of transport for stolen goods (Felson & Eckert, 2018, pp. 55–56). Motor vehicles also made for adverse environmental conditions, including in both town centres and residential areas, with problems of noise, pollution, speeding, hooning, congestion and parking violations. More recently, failure to regulate e-scooters has generated a new form of urban blight with dumped scooters on footpaths and friction between scooter riders and motorists and pedestrians (Cassidy, 2022).

MAKING ROADS SAFE

Looking at the very basic data outlined above, these problems would seem to be overwhelming. However, again, the science of crime prevention, when linked in with a variety of wider system standards, provides a set of relatively simple and easy interventions which are guaranteed to make enormous improvements in people's relationships with transport—whether as drivers, passengers or pedestrians. The key challenge, as usual, is to engage politicians, who often prioritise individual freedom over public safety (Bates et al., 2010).

A key overall road safety strategy is to greatly reduce speeds. For example, a standard of 50 kph has emerged for residential areas in many places but it has been argued that this should be much lower for adequate protection 'where people walk, bike, live and play' (World Health Organization, 2023, p. 35). Speed cameras have been a major influence on reduced road tolls, although they work best with a package of measures within an enforcement pyramid. For example, from late 1989 to 1990, the state of Victoria in Australia—a pioneer jurisdiction—introduced 60 automated speed cameras along with a publicity campaign, improved signage, lowered speed limits, increased automatic licence suspension (to 20 kph over the speed limit) and increased licence demerit points (Bourne & Cooke, 1993). At the same time, the existing small red light camera program was augmented with 20 additional cameras and random breath testing (RBT) was expanded. The new Coordinated Road Safety Strategy was necessitated by an increase in crashes, with 796 fatalities in the 12 months to September 1989 and approximately 10,000 hospitalisations (pp. 177–178) The evaluation showed that, over three years, the percentage of vehicles exceeding speed limits declined by 78%, collisions reduced by 25%, fatalities by 47% and injuries by 41%. Reduced costs for hospitalisations, lost productivity and property damage were put at AU$300 million in the first year (p. 188). A survey put driver support for the program at 80% (p. 190).

Speed camera effects illustrate the fact that road safety is an area where calibrated enforcement strategies can be extremely effective because most drivers have a high stake in conformity (Homel, 1993). Their employment and lifestyles are often dependent on having a licence and a registered vehicle. Most drivers will therefore curb tendencies towards illegal behaviour in response to warnings and smaller penalties. This is also illustrated by the effects of RBT to reduce alcohol-impaired driving. As one example, it was estimated that over a ten-year-period, starting from December 1982, RBT in New South Wales prevented 6,742 serious crashes and 1,487 fatal crashes (Henstridge, Homel & Mackay, 1997, p. 104). To optimise a general deterrent effect, RBT, and similar interventions, must be 'highly visible, ubiquitous, unavoidable and unpredictable', with no discretion exercised by police (Homel, 1993, p. 285). A range of technologies is available to improve both safety and security—including lane departure alerts, rearview cameras, roll bars, speed limiters, mobile phone and seatbelt detection cameras, tracking devices and code locks— but as with the early successes with security devices, such as steering column locks, these have to be mandated to have a large beneficial effect (Webb, 1997).

One option to deal with traffic problems in high pedestrian zones and attract more users is to close off streets, or severely restrict motor vehicle access, by constructing open street malls. A useful overlapping idea is that of the'15-minute city', where all essential services are within 15 minutes walking or cycling distance of residents (Henley et al., 2023). Open malls can become vibrant centres of commerce, entertainment and recreation where people do not have to worry about the noise, pollution and insecurity caused by motor vehicles. At the same time, this process needs to be carefully managed because, as we have seen previously, increased visitor numbers can attract predators. Developments like these require comprehensive crime prevention and security management plans and regular audits to ensure the best set of strategies is at work to optimise order and safety. The presence of human security providers is likely essential—as is common in Business Improvement Districts (Chapter 4).

Disorderly conduct in pedestrian areas can also come from skateboarders, cyclists and e-scooter riders. Regulation of these devices needs to fit different circumstances, but in many locations, governments need to take much stronger protective measures. While the use of e-devices on roads—frequently illegally—represents a major hazard to the driver, their use on footpaths represents a nuisance and hazard for pedestrians, especially vulnerable persons such as children and the elderly (National Transport Commission, 2020). There is a good case for complete jurisdiction-wide bans on e-scooters and e-skateboards, given the inherent dangers posed by these highly exposed and unstable devices. One intermediate measure is to exclude all wheeled vehicles in areas with high rates of foot traffic, which provides maximum safety and comfort for pedestrians. Pedestrian-friendly physical barriers can force riders to stop, observe signage and revert to pushing their devices or riding around a restricted area. Other measures include low speed limits—such as 10 kph in pedestrian areas and 25 kph on bike paths (National Transport Commission, 2020, p. 23)—with the obvious need for clear signage and adequate enforcement. Additional options include built-in speed limits on vehicles and compulsory helmets. Overall, wherever possible, it is best to separate (1) motor vehicles from (2) pushbikes and e-scooters and (3) pedestrians.

CASE STUDIES

The following six more in-depth case studies demonstrate large reductions in crime problems and improvements in transport systems with the deployment of relatively simple situational interventions.

Improving Public Transport in the Netherlands

The 1960s to the 1980s saw increases in fare evasion, violence and vandalism on the Netherlands' public transport system. The increase in crime was associated with budget cuts and removal of conductors (van Andel, 1989, p. 47). The installation of additional doors on trams—to allow for faster passenger turnover—also enlarged opportunities for fare dodging. In response, the Ministry of Transport and Public Works employed approximately 1,200 'Safety, Information and Control' officers—termed VICs—in three cities. The VICs, who began working in 1984, patrolled carriages and public areas, checking tickets. From 1985, bus drivers were required to check for tickets as passengers boarded through the front door.

Evaluation of the fare evasion component of the project occurred through a survey of passengers and staff, and random checks on passengers. The results were somewhat complex across three modes of transport and three cities. Overall, large reductions were found in the first year, with further drops in most cases in the following years. The largest identified reductions in fare evasion in the first year were on the Amsterdam Metro, from 23.5% of passengers to 6.5% (−17%), and on Rotterdam buses, from 14.1% to 2.4% (−11.7%) (pp. 50–51). The Hague tram system, where VICs could not impose fines, had an initial drop but without subsequent falls. Surveys revealed that passengers were aware of the increased inspections. They also supported the changes as improving the fairness of the system. Staff were also supportive.

Despite these improvements, reported feelings of safety involved only small positive changes. However, observations of violent incidents by passengers declined over one year from 11 to 3%. Direct victimisation reportedly declined from 5 to 2%. Some modest reductions were noted in incidents of graffiti and vandalism. The overall quality of public transport and customers service was deemed to have improved in passenger surveys. The changed boarding procedures on buses involved a delay factor, which required the assignment of extra buses, although customers were reportedly happy with the procedures. The VIC program cost about three times the money that was saved, but the various improvements were seen as justifying the outlay (p. 55). One notable feature of the program was a social justice component in the employment of VICs. This was described by van Andel (1989, p. 49) as follows:

> The recruitment campaign was geared to employing unemployed people aged 19-28 and every effort was made to ensure that women and ethnic minorities were well-represented in the intake. There was a good response to the campaign. Requirements were low, but employees had to be able to cope with unfriendly passengers and fare-dodgers: in the end, only one in ten applicants could actually be recruited as a VIC, many proving unsuitable for lack of the required social skills. Of those taken on, 50 per cent had been unemployed, 30 per cent were women, and 25 per cent came from ethnic minority groups... All VICs received short (2-3 month) training comprising a number of courses in criminal law and legal theory and practical exercises in ticket inspection. In general the VICs performed well in their new function.

In cases of conflict, VICs had access to rapid response support teams, including police where necessary.

Victoria's Travel Safe Program

A Travel Safe program in Victoria, Australia, was introduced in the early 1990s to address problems of assaults, vandalism and intimidating and offensive behaviour on the public transport system—covering trains, trams and buses. The network was also plagued with problems of cancelled services, negative media and reduced patronage (Carr & Spring, 1993). Travel Safe was an initiative of the Public Transport Corporation, which deployed improved data for diagnostics, community consultation (mainly through a 'consultative community forum') and advice from experts (p. 149). Out of this process, the following main interventions were implemented:

1. Rapid removal of graffiti and litter, and rapid repair of vandalised property, to improve positive perceptions of the transport system and deny benefits to graffiti offenders;
2. Installation of security devices such as security phones, better lighting (including at bus and tram shelters) and CCTV;
3. High security in stabling yards,
4. Greater circulation and visibility of staff amongst passengers;
5. Increased security guard presence, and increased guards and police at higher-risk times and places;
6. A personal escort service for passengers to parked cars and
7. Community volunteers involved in the removal of physical signs of incivilities and in landscaping in order to increase a sense of ownership.

The results after two years of the program included a reduction of crimes against the person, mainly assaults, by 42% from an average of 57.3 to 33.1 incidents per month. At one stage during 1990, the number of broken train windows averaged 700 per week. This declined to 110 per week in 1992 (−84%). Graffiti 'hits' also declined significantly. Services were more reliable, and the availability of trains increased in peak periods from 65–70% to 98%. Unfortunately, before and after data were not provided on commuters' experiences of the system.

CCTV in King's Lynne and Carpark Crime

CCTV cameras were introduced into different parts of the town centre of King's Lynn in England in 1992 (Brown, 1995). A monitoring station was located in the local authority premises. The station was staffed by private security officers and functioned 24/7. The monitoring staff relayed observations to a police communications centre. The staff were also able to send camera images to the police centre. The police communications centre staff assessed the calls and made decisions on police dispatches to incidents. Arrests for wanted persons could also be activated this way. The system operated on a two-way basis in that police would send requests for information to the monitoring centre. Recordings could also be checked for evidence in investigations.

The program involved 19 cameras, which were concentrated on ground-level carparks subject to problems of theft of motor vehicles, theft from motor vehicles and damage to vehicles. The cameras also viewed adjacent venues and thoroughfares. They were also used to monitor litter and parking and also flooding of the local river. The system was funded by a small surcharge on parking tickets and funds from local businesses.

The evaluation by Brown (1995) examined rolling averages per quarter for five crime categories across four quarters before the introduction of the carpark area cameras and seven quarters following. These data were compared to those for the remainder of the smaller Police Division and the remainder of the larger Police Force area. Overall, the evaluation identified large reductions in crime post-intervention. Theft from vehicles had been declining before the intervention, reaching an average of 13 cases per quarter. However, the number declined from 13 to approximately five at the end of the final quarter (−62%). Theft of vehicles had also been declining ahead of the intervention. However, the camera system most likely contributed to further reductions, almost eliminating the problem. In the final quarter pre-intervention, the average was seven thefts of vehicles, with a figure of one at the end the evaluation period (−86%). Large reductions post-intervention were also identified in burglary, and also wounding and assault, with a moderate fall in criminal damage. The trends for the comparative areas involved moderate increases and moderate falls. The evaluation also found that the cameras were associated with 80 arrests for property offences and just under 100 arrests for public order crimes. Of additional note was the fact that the screening system greatly reduced the number of unnecessary urgent calls to police.

Reducing Vehicle Thefts in a Carpark in Dover

This case study from the early 1980s was focused on the theft of cars from a multi-tiered carpark in the coastal town of Dover in England (Poyner, 1997). The carpark consisted of 11 split-level floors with approximately 400 spaces. Apart from high rates of vehicle theft, there were also problems of theft from vehicles, loitering, vandalism and urinating in the stairwell. The facility was open access and open exit with a pay-and-display payment system. Diagnostics suggested that easy access and anonymity were major facilitators of crime. Random inspections by local council officers during the day and private security patrols at night appeared to have little effect. An added problem was that numerous holiday makers used the facility and had their vehicles stolen, contributing to reputational damage to the town.

The intervention consisted of 'a package of measures ... developed by local officials in consultation with a police crime prevention officer' (Poyner, 1997, p. 158). The package represented a fairly minimalist and low-cost set of environmental changes, introduced in late 1983, consisting of the following:

1. Wire mesh was installed at the ground level between the outside walls and ceilings;
2. A self-closing steel door was installed at the pedestrian entrance so it functioned only as an exit, forcing pedestrians to enter via the main driveway;
3. Lighting was upgraded at the main entrance and stairway exit and
4. An office was installed at the main entrance and rented to a taxi company who had staff on duty from early in the morning to late at night.

The main intended effects therefore were to restrict entry and improve natural surveillance.

The evaluation by Poyner (1997) reported that thefts declined by 83% from 38 cars in the two years 1982–1983, up to and including the installation of the interventions, to seven in the following two years 1984–1985 (p. 161). Smaller numbers of thefts, occurring in nearby ground-level carparks with better natural surveillance, also declined in this period but at a lower rate—suggesting an absence of displacement and a possible diffusion of benefits.

As with many case studies like this, lack of data from offenders makes it difficult to identify the exact nature of a cause-and-effect relationship. However, a reasonable inference is that the changes helped deter offenders by increasing the effort and risks of offending via target hardening and enhanced guardianship. Of interest is the fact that theft from cars declined but at a much lower rate: from 42 to 33 incidents. The tentative explanation for this was that numerous thefts from vehicles were perpetrated by offenders in vehicles who carried the stolen property away in their cars. This was much more difficult to prevent with the limited measures that were adopted. Finally, although no numbers were provided, when it came to the other problems of crime and disorder on the premises, vandalism was reportedly 'greatly reduced' to the extent that the financial cost of the works was recouped in the first year (p. 158). Usage of the carpark also increased.

A Security Bike Patrol in a Commuter Carpark in Vancouver

Barclay et al. (1997) describe a very short, but nonetheless instructive, 'experiment' in preventing motor vehicle theft by deploying parapolice to patrol a carpark. The location was the Scott Road SkyTrain Park-and-Ride commuter facility in Vancouver, which provided 1,532 parking spaces and access to buses and trains. The site was characterised by high rates of vehicle theft, with an average of 24 thefts per month. The British Columbia Insurance Corporation was reportedly making payouts of CA$40,000 on average per month. The site was described as 'an ideal location for the crime of motor vehicle theft' (p. 146). It was open 24 hours; it had multiple open access points; it was unfenced, flat and open with no observation points; and there were no shops. Most offenders were engaged in joyriding.

After rejecting a proposal for a major security upgrade on cost grounds, British Columbia Transit agreed to test a mobile patrol for one month, funded by the BC Insurance Corporation. A private security company was engaged to provide four security guards, dressed in hi-viz, who randomly patrolled the grounds in pairs on pushbikes from 7 am to 7 pm Monday to Friday. The appearance of the officers was similar to that of police bike patrol officers in Vancouver. The bikes allowed for surveillance over the roofs of the cars and quick access to any location. The riders were also highly visible to commuters and offenders. To optimise deterrence, the patrols were preceded for three weeks by widespread publicity in local media outlets.

The evaluation of the project was focused on the numbers of stolen vehicles, with a large reduction associated with the intervention, beginning with the publicity campaign and continuing on after the patrols were stopped. According to Barclay et al. (1997, p. 148),

> During the eight-month pre-test phase, 192 cars were reported stolen. This was an average of 24 cars per month. During the test month (April), only three cars were reported stolen [-88%]. Theft of autos remained lower than average during the post experimental phase, with only three cars reportedly stolen during May and 13 stolen reported in June.

In four comparison sites, motor vehicle theft numbers remained largely the same. With no data from offenders, commuters or patrol officers, it was assumed that a general deterrent effect was the main influence on the reduction in offences at the experimental site. Of some interest is the initial fall in thefts associated with the publicity campaign—from a spike of 12 in the fortnight prior to the campaign down to three at the end of the campaign (p. 150). Given this occurred before the patrols were operationalised, the effect was explained in terms of an 'anticipatory diffusion' of benefits (p. 143). There was also an apparent residual deterrent effect and temporal diffusion of benefits, after the patrols were stopped (p. 151).

Stopping Graffiti on the Subway System: New York City's Clean Car Program

The New York City subway system in the 1970s and early 1980s was characterised by extensive and highly visible graffiti and vandalism. Concerted efforts to arrest the mainly juvenile offenders, force offenders to clean carriages, introduce graffiti-defeating paints and target harden the enormous expanse of tracks had failed. Offenders were motivated by a subculture of peer esteem around tagging. According to Sloan-Howitt and Kelling (1997), 'The New York City government's and the New York City Transit Authority's (NYCTA) striking attempts—and failures—to outwit these youths and deter their spectacular defacement of public property only served to embolden the graffitists' (p. 240). Graffiti and vandalism drove fear of crime and a sense that the legitimate authorities had lost control, which reduced patronage, especially at off-peak times. Police evidence indicated that offender involvement in graffiti was a gateway to more serious crimes. The crime problem was also closely associated with a wider problem of inefficiency and disfunction (p. 242):

> Fires were epidemic; subways trains derailed on the average of one every 18 days; in 400 places in the system, track conditions were so bad that train speeds had to be reduced by 75%; and on any given day, a third of the subway fleet was out of service during the morning rush hours.

In 1984, in an effort to short circuit the problem, a new President of NYCTA introduced a highly innovative and daring 'Clean Car Program' (CCP). According to Sloan-Howitt & Kelling, 1997, p. 243):

> The NYCTA's CCP was based on a relatively simple idea: Once a car was cleaned and entered into the program, it would never again leave a storage maintenance, or lay-by area with graffiti. Its implementation was difficult and included risks: If it meant keeping a car out of service, even during rush hours (as it did 10 times during the program's 5 years), so be it. No one would "get up" again on cars entered into the program.

At the same time, the cleaning program was introduced progressively to ensure there was no excessive disruption. Some additional features included lighting upgrades and 24-hour personnel in fenced cleaning yards. As the program expanded, police, including undercover officers, engaged in more focused deterrence and incapacitation strategies by riding cars at high-risk times and targeting known repeat offenders for arrest. Police reportedly also sought support from the parents of repeat offenders and threatened to take action in the civil courts for restitution.

The program evaluation consisted primarily of counts of clean cars. By early 1989, five years after the program began, 'the trains were graffiti-free' (Sloan & Kelling, 1997, p. 245). If this is true, then it evidences one of the most successful crime prevention programs on record, with a 100% reduction in the core problem. The program also ticks many of the boxes for best practices in crime prevention. Although it included an offender-oriented component, this was focused on repeat offenders and, over the long-term, arrests for graffiti and vandalism offences declined from a peak of 237 for felonies and 2681 for misdemeanours in 1984 to 114 and 974 respectively in 1988 (p. 247). It also represented a shift from a police-led law enforcement approach to innovation and leadership by third-party place managers—through an internal facilities maintenance program with police in a support role (p. 248).

From a situational prevention perspective, the main strategy struck directly at the primary motivation of offenders by removing the rewards for their actions (Sloan-Howitt & Kelling, 1997, p. 248):

> The CCP simply deprived youths of the satisfaction of having their work seen. Certainly not immediately, but slowly, however, graffitists learned that tagging trains entered into the program was hopeless—the work would be in vain, it would never be seen.

By the middle of the program cleaning crews were greatly reduced as 'the incidence of new graffiti had dropped to almost nothing' (p. 249). Importantly, the program represented a willingness to experiment, to try new things, within a problem-solving framework. This included experiments with different cleaning products and tools. The primary measurement of success was also highly innovative in counting towards an ideal state—clean cars—rather than reduced criminal offences. The audits showed that the number of clean cars increased from 400 in 1984 to the 'entire fleet' of 6,245 in 1989 (p. 246). Of additional importance was the fact the innovative new President of the network, with a personal interest in Graffiti abatement, David Gunn, took office at a time when 'the financial means and … political will' were available to support the new program (p. 245).

Despite the apparent success of the Clean Car Program, the evaluation by Sloan and Kelling (1997) lacked some important sources of information. There were no commuter or broader citizen perception and experience surveys reported, and no data was included on possible increases in usage of the system. The were also no financial cost–benefit data, although cleaning costs must have reduced substantially over time. Data were also missing in the various case dispositions and their impacts trialled with the arrested repeat offenders.

Conclusion

The evidence assembled from diverse sources in this chapter shows that safe efficient and clean transport systems are not a fantasy but an achievable goal for public authorities. Making the most of technology to automate surveillance and enforcement systems is likely to yield large benefits. Other beneficial situational measures, evident in the case studies, include increasing visible formal and informal guardianship, restricting access, target hardening, reducing rewards and improving image. At the same time, success in this area requires an overarching approach of genuine concern for the well-being of commuters and pedestrians and the adoption of a data-driven experimental problem-solving approach. While doing this, authorities need to ensure they are consultative and transparent with all aspects of the planning and implementation processes.

REFERENCES

Barclay, P., Buckley, J., Brantingham, P., Brantingham, P., & Whin-Yates, T. (1997). Preventing auto theft in commuter lots: A bike patrol in Vancouver. In R. Clarke (Ed.), *Situational crime prevention: Successful case studies* (pp. 143–156). Harrow and Heston.

Bates, L., Soole, D., & Watson, B. (2016). The effectiveness of traffic policing in reducing traffic crashes. In T. Prenzler (Ed.), *Policing and security in practice: Challenges and achievements* (pp. 90–109). Palgrave-Macmillan.

Bates, L., Watson, B., & King, M. (2010). Mobility and safety are conflicting goals for transport policy makers when making decisions about graduated driver licensing. *International Journal of Health Promotion and Education*, 48(2), 46–51.

Bourne, M., & Cooke, R. (1993). Victoria's speed camera program. In R. Clarke (Ed.), *Crime prevention studies* (pp. 177–192). Criminal Justice Press.

Brown, B. (1995). *CCTV in Town Centres: Three Case Studies*. Home Office (United Kingdom).

Carr, K., & Spring, G. (1993). Public transport safety: A Community right and a communal responsibility. In R. Clarke (Ed.), *Crime prevention studies* (pp. 147–155). Criminal Justice Press.

Cassidy, C. (2022, July 23). Solution or hazard? Australia's e-scooter debate gains speed, but the rules are a mess. *Guardian Australia*. https://www.theguardian.com/australia-news/2022/jul/23/solution-or-hazard-australias-e-scooter-debate-gains-speed-but-the-rules-are-a-mess

Felson, M., & Eckert, M. (2018). *Crime and everyday life: A brief introduction*. SAGE.

Henley, J., Burgen, S., & O'Carroll, L. (2023). Bollards and 'superblocks': How Europe's cities are turning on the car. *The Guardian*. https://www.theguardian.com/cities/2023/dec/18/bollards-and-superblocks-how-europes-cities-are-turning-on-the-car

Henstridge, J., Homel, R., & Mackay, P. (1997). *The long-term effects of random breath testing in four Australian states*. Department of Transport and Regional Development (Australian Government).

Homel, R. (1993). Random breath testing in Australia: Getting it to work according to specifications. *Addiction, 88*(Supplement), 27S–33S.

National Transport Commission (Australia). (2020). *Barriers to the safe use of personal mobility devices*. https://www.ntc.gov.au/sites/default/files/assets/files/NTC-Decision-RIS-PMDs.pdf

Poyner, B. (1997). Situational crime prevention in two parking facilities. In R. Clarke (Ed.), *Situational crime prevention: Successful case studies* (pp. 157–166). Harrow and Heston.

Prenzler, T. (2018). Aviation security in Australia. In J. Szyliowicz & L. Zamparini (Eds.), *Air transport security: Issues, challenges and national policies* (pp. 245–262). Edward Elgar.

Prenzler, T., & Sarre, R. (2021). Community safety, crime prevention and 21st century policing. In P. Birch, P. Kennedy, & E. Kruger (Eds.), *Australian policing: Critical issues in 21st century police practice* (pp. 283–298). Routledge.

Sloan-Howitt, M., & Kelling, G. (1997). Subway graffiti in New York City: "Getting' up" vs, "Meaning' it and Cleanin' it". In R. Clarke (Ed.), *Situational crime prevention: Successful case studies* (pp. 242–249). Harrow and Heston.

van Andel, H. (1989). Crime prevention that works: The care of public transport in the Netherlands. *British Journal of Criminology, 29*(1), 47–56.

Webb, B. (1997). Steering column locks and motor vehicle theft: Evaluations from three countries. In R. Clarke (Ed.), *Situational crime prevention: Successful case studies* (pp. 46–58). Harrow and Heston.

World Health Organization. (2023). *Global status report on road safety 2023*. World Health Organization

CHAPTER 6

Reducing Public Intoxication and Alcohol-Related Crime in Entertainment Precincts

Abstract Entertainment areas are major attractors and facilitators of crime, especially where alcohol is involved. However, evaluated intervention programs have yielded numerous best practice principles to prevent alcohol-related crime and minimise harm. Likely beneficial strategies include responsible service procedures, venue opening hour limits, coordinated transport and security officer professionalisation. Illustrative cases include the Surfers Paradise Safety Action Project, the Geelong Venues Against Violence Accord, reduced closing hours in Newcastle (Australia) and the STAD Project (STockholm prevents Alcohol and Drug problems).

Keywords Responsible service of alcohol · Closing hours · Liquor law enforcement · Crowding

CONTEXTS

There is a range of harms associated with excess alcohol consumption in publicly accessible venues such as pubs and clubs. Problems, like arguments and fights, can occur inside venues, and these can spill outside onto footpaths and streets. Common harms include injuries and fatalities from accidents and assaults, harassment and sexual harassment, public urination and vomiting and a general atmosphere of disorder and intimidation. Alcohol can have a disinhibiting effect on users and also impairs cognition (Newbury-Birch & Ferguson, 2023, p. 9). Both conditions contribute to increased vulnerability to offending and victimisation. More specific, interactive, causes of alcohol-related misbehaviour in entertainment areas include male aggression and peer pressure, profit-driven sales policies, boredom and overcrowding, under-enforcement by liquor licensing authorities, negligence and incitement by security staff and lack of infrastructure such as public toilets and joined up transport (Homel et al., 1992, 2004; Miller et al., 2012a, 2012b, 2012c).

In tackling alcohol-related harms, there is a great deal that authorities can do. Local government has a key role, although state and national authorities also need to set up a regulatory context that makes it as easy as possible for local authorities to enact effective place-based interventions with local police, regulators and venue managers. Examples of broader preventive measures include restrictions or bans on advertising alcohol, age limits on the purchase of alcohol and random breath testing of drivers (Babor et al., 2003; Loxley et al, 2004; Newbury-Birch & Ferguson, 2023). Reducing the availability of alcohol is a key measure highlighted in the literature (Miller et al., 2021; Stockwell, 2010). Adequate pricing through taxation is also endorsed by international reviews as a major means of reducing consumption (Miller et al., 2012b, 2012c; Newbury-Birch & Ferguson, 2023; Stockwell, 2010). As an example of the latter, a study in Australia's Northern Territory tracked the effect of a 5% increase in the price of a standard alcoholic drink over four years, finding that the change was associated with 129 fewer alcohol-related deaths and 1,300 hospital admissions, saving approximately AU$123 million (Stockwell, 2010, p. 29).

SPECIFIC STRATEGIES

The following section discusses 12 strategies applicable in entertainment areas and venues. They involve situational and CPTED measures such as setting rules, controlling access, facilitating compliance, reducing emotional arousal, avoiding disputes, reducing frustrations, neutralising peer pressure and extending formal and informal guardianship, alongside the application of an enforcement pyramid.

Responsible Service of Alcohol

'Responsible Service of Alcohol' (RSA)—or 'responsible serving programs' (Homel et al., 1997, p. 41)—involves a set of rules for managing the sale of alcohol to minimise the chances of intoxication and harm. RSA can be applied through jurisdictionally based training packages, with certification required for persons who work in roles associated with the supply of alcohol. Key elements of RSA include authenticating age-related identification, recognising signs of intoxication and diplomatically refusing more drinks and intervening to de-escalate aggressive behaviour.

Stockwell's (2010) review of Australian and Canadian evidence for 'what works' in community-wide efforts to prevent the problem of violence in and around licensed premises found strong evidence in support of Responsible Service of Alcohol training programs for managers and bar staff when part of a comprehensive strategy—including liquor law enforcement (below). The Surfers Paradise Safety Action Project is one well-documented example of a successful intervention program based on the implementation of an RSA code (discussed in detail in the case studies section below). Other examples include the Stockholm Prevents Alcohol and Drug Problems Project (case studies section below), the Safer Bars program in Toronto (Graham et al., 2004) and the Sacramento Neighborhood Alcohol Prevention Project (SNAPP) (Treno et al., 2007).

Lockout Laws and Closing Hours

'Lockouts' prohibit patrons from entering licensed premises after a designated time while permitting the sale and consumption of alcohol to continue inside. Closing hours shut down all activities and require patrons to exit the premises. Closing hours can be accompanied by a 'last drinks' sales window, such as half an hour before closing. These restrictions are designed to reduce intoxication and manage the movement of intoxicated patrons by staggering the times that patrons leave the premises.

Reviews of lockout laws have found mixed results, suggesting they might not work on their own but might be effective within a package of measures, including regulating 'last drinks' (Nepal et al., 2018; Taylor et al., 2019; Wilkinson et al., 2016). Nepal et al. (2018) assessed eight studies of lock outs. Two showed reductions in assaults, one found reductions exclusively within licensed premises, two reported increases in assaults and three indicated no effects. In a study in Queensland, Taylor et al. (2019) investigated the impacts of liquor trading restrictions in the form of (1) limited opening hours to 2 am and mandatory ID scanners (below) for Safe Night Precincts and (2) a 3 am lockout for other venues and a ban on sales of high percentage alcohol drinks after midnight for venues with a 60 + patron capacity. While the researchers found a reduction in serious late-night assaults in Queensland's largest Safe Night Precinct of Fortitude Valley, they found no significant difference between changes in serious assaults for other precincts or local government areas.

New South Wales has also been the site of innovation in this area. In response to public outcry regarding the deaths of two young men assaulted in Kings Cross, Sydney, on New Year's Eve 2013, restrictions on licensed premises were introduced in 2014 to curb alcohol-related violence (Menéndez et al., 2015). Reforms to the state Liquor Act included the following (pp. 1–2):

1. 1.30 am lockouts at hotels, registered clubs, nightclubs and karaoke bars in two designated areas: the Sydney CBD Entertainment Precinct and Kings Cross Precinct;
2. 3.00 am cessation of alcohol service in venues in these Precincts;
3. A freeze on new liquor licences and approvals for existing licences across the Sydney CBD Entertainment Precinct and continuation of the existing freeze in the Kings Cross Precinct;
4. A ban on takeaway alcohol sales after 10.00 pm across NSW;
5. The extension of temporary and long-term banning orders issued to designated 'troublemakers' to prevent them entering most licensed premises in the Kings Cross and Sydney CBD entertainment precincts;
6. The introduction of a new risk based licence fee for all licensed premises in which the annual fee payable by a particular venue depends upon its licence type, compliance history and trading hours;
7. The suspension of online responsible service of alcohol training.

The evaluation by Menéndez et al. (2015) identified substantial reductions in assaults in Kings Cross (−32%) and Sydney CBD entertainment precincts (−40%) following the reforms, with little evidence of displacement. A smaller reduction of 9% occurred across the rest of New South Wales. The results were muddied somewhat by uncertainty around the effects of different interventions (e.g., banning orders vs. lockouts) and possible reductions in patronage due to adverse publicity. Business owners and staff campaigned against the changes, reporting reductions in patronage between 20 and 50%.

One of the apparently more successful early lockout programs occurred in Newcastle, New South Wales, in 2008 (Kypri et al., 2011). The intervention (see case studies section below) was associated with a one-third reduction in night-time assaults. However, a follow-up study indicated that the reduced closing time, from 5 am to 3.30, was probably more effective than the lockouts (Kypri et al., 2014). Rossow and Nostrom's (2012) review of nine studies found a strong association between changes in trading hours and violence. Extended or unrestricted closing hours tended to be associated with increased violence, and restricted hours tended to be associated with decreased violence. In their primary research in Norway, involving 18 cities, they found that a one-hour increase in trading hours was associated with a 16% increase in assaults, while a one-hour reduction in hours was associated with a 20% reduction in assaults. In Geneva, Switzerland, alcohol-related hospitalisations fell by 25–40% across different age cohorts of young persons after off-license premises were required to stop selling alcohol between 9 pm and 7 am (Wicki & Gmel, 2011). Finally, a study in Melbourne found that 'each additional high-alcohol hour that a venue can be open for is associated with a 72% increase in the number of recorded assaults' (Miller et al., 2021, p. 1298). (See also Huckle et al., 2020).

Liquor Law Enforcement

Legislated restrictions on the sale and supply of alcohol constitute an essential first step in reducing alcohol-related harm. Legislation can embody a broad range of principles and requirements, including Responsible Service of Alcohol requirements, closing hours, use of ID scanners, noise levels and numbers of licensed security officers, to name a few. However, laws achieve little unless they are enforced, and under-enforcement, or under-regulation, is cited repeatedly in the literature as a major factor in violence (e.g., Babor, 2010). Enlargement of rules in combination with committed enforcement are features of successful violence reduction case studies (below; also Graham & Homel, 2012, p. 205ff; Treno et al., 2007).

The enforcement process can involve a substantial element of self-regulation, encouraged through voluntary agreements such as stakeholder accords, but there also needs to be a strong independent enforcement component involving government regulators—primarily liquor licence authorities and police—to ensure there is an adequate deterrent effect and willingness to shut down non-compliant premises when necessary. Application of the enforcement pyramid (Chapter 2) is part of the best practice model: stepping up from communication and warnings to fines and shut downs as necessary. Rigour and accountability in enforcement also need to be demonstrated through published impact data from audits, inspections and prosecutions; including statistics on assaults, injuries and disorder; with data from customers, staff and managers (Babor et al., 2003; Loxley et al., 2004). Given the enormous financial costs of alcohol-related violence, investments in enforcement should be cost-effective. For example, in the area of road safety, a study in the United States estimated that every dollar spent on liquor law enforcement saved US$260 in reduced alcohol-related crashes (McKnight & Streff, 1994).

Enforcement also needs to include a randomised component so that regulated entities do not have time to present as compliant and then return to non-compliance following an inspection. Compliance monitoring can be enhanced through the use of undercover and covert testing, including 'mystery shopper' programs that audit staff responses to ostensibly intoxicated customers or under-age liquor purchase requests (McKnight & Streff, 1994; Prenzler et al., 2022, p. 15). Enforcement should also be intelligence-driven in prioritising attention to the locations and causes of alcohol-related harm based on data collection systems. For example, the innovative New South Wales Alcohol Linking Project demonstrated a reduction in harm associated with licensed venues through the systematic collection by police of basic information about where an individual arrested for an alcohol-related offence purchased their last drink (Wiggers et al., 2004). The data were used to target police audits of premises. The audits had 'a harm reduction rather than strictly compliance focus' (p. 359). However, follow-up visits were also used to facilitate compliance. Surveys showed that the program received support from police and licensees, and an impact assessment indicated a 22% reduction in alcohol-related crime over a six-month period.

ID Scanners and Banned Patron Lists

ID scanners involve entry screening and reduce anonymity, potentially deterring offenders by increasing the risk of detection. Scanners are intended to identify fraudulent IDs and also have the potential to incapacitate repeat offenders by preventing entry to premises (Lindsay, 2012; Miller et al., 2019). While banning violence-prone individuals would seem to make sense, the evidence for the effectiveness of this approach is mixed at best. In fact, Miller et al.'s (2012b) review of initiatives to reduce alcohol-related violence was unable to find evidence to support both ID scanners and banned patron lists, although a survey of patrons and stakeholder sources showed strong support and police reported that they were a helpful means of solving crimes.

More recently, in a study in Victoria, Australia, Curtis et al. (2022) found that bans appeared to increase anti-social behaviour. However, some support for bans is provided by a recent study from Western Australia by Farmer et al. (2023). The authors examined available data on the impacts of 'police-imposed barring notices ... introduced in WA in January 2011 ... issued in response to alcohol-related disorderly behaviours in/around licensed venues' (p. 1). Under this system, recipients can be banned from venues for up to one year. During 9.5 years, from 2011 to mid-2020, police issued 4,023 notices (p. 6). The authors compared assault offences, including alcohol-involved offences, recorded by police for this period with those occurring in the preceding four years. The evaluation report was unable to show a clear cause-and-effect relationship between bans and reduced violence, and the report did not specify pre- and post- offence averages. However, time series data indicated a modest downward trend in relevant offences post-intervention, and the following summary indicates some support for a positive relationship (p. 17):

> The most significant reductions (immediate and ongoing) following the introduction of barring notices related to non-family assault offences marked with an alcohol flag; common assault offences marked with an alcohol flag; and assault offences recorded as taking place on pathways (which includes areas around licensed premises). All reflect behaviours that are directly relevant to the purpose, location and intended application of barring notices.

Licensed Venue Density and Capacity

The idea of limiting the geographical density of liquor outlets has been supported by a series of studies showing strong links between venue density and violence (e.g., Campbell et al., 2009; Gruenewald et al., 2006; Livingston, 2008). The problem can extend to venue capacity. For example, a study in Melbourne found that 'venues with maximum capacities between 501 and 1000 are 6.1 times more likely to have an assault recorded compared with venues with a maximum capacity between 0 and 100' (Miller et al., 2021, p. 1298). However, the implications of these findings do not necessarily go against the idea of special entertainment precincts. A study in Western Australia by Liang and Chikritzhs (2011) suggested that violence associated with venue density could be worsened by close venue proximity and crowding inside venues. The Miller et al. (2021) study highlighted the fact that the large majority of venues were able to serve alcohol without assaults occurring, supporting the view that problems usually relate to a small proportion of venues. Overall then, the findings lend some support to a policy encouraging smaller venues, under a responsible management regime, along with focused monitoring of larger venues.

Reducing Crowding

Crowding in entertainment areas with alcohol service has been shown to be a major precipitator of violence (Homel et al., 1992). Patron limits are therefore a key component of regulation. At the same time, crowding and conflict can be reduced by changes to the layout and operation of venues (Macintyre & Homel, 1997). Adequate staffing can reduce crowding at bars. Comfortable and quiet areas for conversation facilitate relaxation, reducing frustration and emotional arousal. Layouts should also ensure dance floors, bars, seating areas and toilets are adequately separated to avoid patrons crossing paths.

Patron Mix

Diversity within venues might help reduce alcohol-related violence—mainly perpetrated by young males. Lindsay's (2012) study of young drinkers in night-time entertainment venues in regional towns and cities in Victoria, Australia, found that the presence of women was observed to have a 'civilising effect' in reducing aggression—particularly where there was a higher ratio of women to men (p. 240). Women can act as 'handlers' in the crime triangle (Chapter 2), in restraining male companions. This suggests the utility of efforts to attract a diversity of patrons, although it should be kept in mind that the Geelong Accord study (below) found that strategies to attract women, such as free entry, appeared to contribute to problems (Felson et al., 1997).

Venue Amenity

A variety of studies have shown correlations between venue amenities, including patron comfort, staff friendliness (including security staff), entertainment and food, on the one hand, and, on the other hand, reduced levels of aggression and violence (e.g., Homel et al., 1992, 2004; Stockwell, 2010). Venue amenity helps reduce frustration and aggression, and the supply of food and entertainment reduces heavy drinking and intoxication. For example, it has been reported that drinking alcohol with a complete meal can reduce alcohol levels in the body by up to 60% (Stockwell, 2010, p. 19). Legislating these nuanced standards is difficult, but they can be written into accord agreements and encouraged as part of a regulatory process focused on licensee responsibility for minimising violence.

Shatterproof Glassware

Rules requiring the service of alcohol in shatterproof glasses—such as polycarbonate glassware (PCG)—are now a commonplace response to problems of violence involving broken glasses and bottles—often referred to as 'glassings'. Impact research in this area has suffered from some limitations, such as inexact data for venues with and without PCG, and injury data that fail to distinguish between accidents and assaults. However, studies on the whole indicate that glass substitutes can contribute to reduced numbers of injuries from both deliberate misuse and accidental breakages and contribute to a safer drinking environment (Clarke, 2020; Forsyth, 2008). Studies have also shown that high-quality PCG attracts support from customers, staff and management. They are also much cheaper to produce and can be manufactured from recycled material (e.g., Anderson et al., 2009).

Behaviour Management and De-escalation Techniques

There is also strong evidence that management and staff training can be effective in reducing violent incidents. In the past, in many locations, security staff have been notorious for failing to protect patrons, provoking violence for entertainment or engaging in assaults (Victorian Community Council Against Violence, 1990). Negligent management has also been part of the mix of intoxication and violence. From that perspective, advanced communication and interpersonal skills are essential to anticipate, prevent, intervene early and de-escalate violence, including through teamwork (Stockwell, 2010). The Canadian Safer Bars program is an example of a successful violence prevention program, involving the following key personnel development component (Graham et al., 2004, p. 31):

> owners/managers completed the risk assessment workbook to identify ways of reducing environmental risks, and 373 staff and owners/managers (84% participation rate) attended a 3-hour training session focused on preventing escalation of aggression, working as a team and resolving problem situations safely.

The risk assessment process covered 92 items, including the floor plan, patron comfort levels and house rules.

Outdoor Seating Areas and Late-Night Dining

After making an exit, patrons of bars and clubs often do not want to head home immediately. This can be attributed to wanting the fun to continue, peer pressure, or lack of public transport (Berkley & Thayer, 2000). Consequently, loitering and drunk and disorderly offences are more likely to occur, with the possibility for further harm if there is a large congregation of intoxicated persons in one place. It has been suggested that seating areas can encourage the dispersal of intoxicated impatient and tired crowds (Berkley & Thayer, 2000)—although these can also facilitate loitering. Late-night dining options also encourage patrons to disperse and/or leave night-time entertainment areas, while providing an opportunity to sober up before heading home. The addition of late-night services such as food vendors, and rest and recovery areas, that do not include alcohol, also provide forms of informal surveillance and guardianship.

Public Transport

Lack of public transport is a widely recognised facilitator of crime problems in night-time entertainment areas (Miller et al., 2012a). Lack of transport can contribute to drink-driving, injuries to intoxicated pedestrians, and increased violence through frustration and boredom (Streker, 2012). Late-night public transport can also bring vulnerable persons and offenders together. A variety of measures can counter these problems, including coordination of buses and trains with closing hours and peak demand, marshals at taxi ranks, security guards on trains and buses, and escorts from stations to carparks (Carr & Spring, 1993; see Victoria's Travel Safe Program in Chapter 5).

CASE STUDIES

The following section provides more detailed accounts of selected intervention studies in entertainment areas where alcohol was a major factor in violence. As noted previously in this book, successful prevention initiatives often involve multiple interventions to address complex crime problems involving different types of crime. This makes it difficult to determine what exactly works in different situations. Nonetheless, successful projects provide clues as to what is worth trialling in other settings, and a package of measures is likely to be maximally effective. The case study approach also allows for some insights into process issues, which can be critical to the long-term success of crime prevention initiatives.

The Surfers Paradise Safety Action Project

This Project was established in 1993 as a multi-partner initiative designed to reduce violence within and around licensed venues in the major tourist area of Surfers Paradise, Australia. Periodic police crackdowns had proven unsuccessful, and mounting community and business concern forced authorities to take action. The initiative came from a criminologist, who obtained cooperation from key stakeholders and a federal grant to support the work as a demonstration project (Homel et al., 1997, p. 44). The project was managed through a steering committee involving the Gold Coast City Council, the state health department, the police, the local chamber of commerce, a tourist promotion body, the liquor regulator and a university research team. A project officer coordinated the day-to-day operations and stakeholder liaison. An initial assessment of the nature and causes of the problem led to the development and implementation of the following interventions (Homel et al., 1997):

1. Enlarged responsible service practices to reduce drinks discounting and service of alcohol to intoxicated individuals and under-age persons,
2. Publication of the responsible service policy,
3. Reduced noise levels,
4. Improved cleanliness,
5. Availability of lower alcohol drinks,
6. Upgraded entertainment,
7. More professional, less aggressive, security staff,
8. More rigorous identification checks,
9. Improved availability of food,
10. Improved access and reduced crowding around bars to reduce situational precipitators of conflict,
11. More public transport.

The project included a Security and Policing Task Group which brought together a range of security-oriented stakeholders including police and venue security providers, with a focus on the areas outside licensed venues. Better training of security staff in de-escalation was a major outcome of the Group's work, along with joint street patrols and introduction of a shuttle bus to assist with transport out of the entertainment area—reducing frustration, violence and drink-driving. Security officers were also deployed at taxi ranks, and venue managers employed more security officers, taking pressure off police.

The project evaluation involved field observations and police-recorded crime. The observations were conducted in 18 nightclubs over two summers in 1993 and 1994 (pre- and post-intervention). These data identified major reductions in incidents of verbal abuse (−82%, from 12.5 to 2.3 per 100 hours of observation) and arguments (−68%, from 7.1 to 2.3 per 100 hours) (Homel et al., 1997, p. 70). Physical assaults declined by 52% as a rate per 100 hours. However, this was not statistically significant given the small numbers involved: 11 and 4 incidents. Police records showed reductions in incidents of 'drunk and disorderly' conduct across comparable five-month periods pre- and post-implementation—from 258 to 146 (−43%)—and assaults—from 50 to 33 (−34%). There was no evidence of displacement of violence or disorder to neighbouring areas. In 1994 the approach was replicated in three cities—Cairns, Townsville and Mackay—with similar positive outcomes (Hauritz et al., 1998; Homel et al., 2004). Across the three sites over two years, observers recorded declines in verbal abuse of 60.4%, arguments of 28.2%, 'challenges/threats' of 40.5%, assaults of 81.2% and male drunkenness of 65.6%.

In Surfers Paradise, the project plan included an 'intensive intervention' period with a major role for the project officer (Homel et al., 1997, p. 76). The idea was then to move from this 'person-dependent' form of management to 'process-dependent' program maintenance by stakeholders, including venue management and the regulator. However, data for 1996 showed that aggression, conflict and violence had largely returned to pre-intervention levels. Stakeholder testimony indicated that the project had fallen apart: 'many licensees were flaunting its provisions in order to secure short-term profits' and the liquor licensing regulator 'failed to discipline the errant operators' (p. 77).

The Geelong Venues Against Violence Accord

The Geelong Venues against Violence Accord began in the late 1980s, described as one of the first liquor accords in the world (Miller et al., 2012a). The Accord involved an agreement between local police, liquor licensees and the state Liquor Licensing Commission to respond to alcohol-fuelled disorder in the Geelong city centre (Felson et al., 1997). Geelong's alcohol-related disorder at the time included public intoxication, under-age and outdoor liquor consumption, intimidation, assaults, property damage, drunk driving, public urination and excessive noise—all in the context of a culture that advocated drinking to excess. Intense competition between pubs and clubs encouraged heavy alcohol consumption through free entry to venues and drink discounting.

According to Felson et al.'s (1997) evaluation, 'Police organised and led the [Accord] process' (p. 126). It also noted that police 'present[ed] the policy to publicans in a non-authoritarian manner', while the police and the Licensing Commission 'maintained a "hidden stick"—the ability to investigate and ultimately close down businesses' (p. 126). The Accord was managed through bi-monthly meetings of a Best Practices

Committee, consisting of police, the Licensing Commission, venue representatives and the City Council. The consultation process led to managers of the 14 main hotels and nightclubs in the area signing up to a voluntary code of practice, summarised as follows (Felson et al., 1997, 123, 125):

1. No free drinks,
2. No drinks promotions,
3. Common minimum pricing,
4. No extended 'happy hour',
5. A cover charge after 11 pm,
6. No free re-entry,
7. No rule exemptions for females,
8. Greater availability of taxis,
9. Non-alcohol-related entertainment for under-age youth on some licensed premises, and
10. Alcohol-free 'blue-light' discos for under-age teenagers.

There was also a focus on enforcement of laws prohibiting public drinking and under-age drinking and laws against false identification cards. A key strategy was to use warnings and seizure of false ID cards before resorting to arrest.

The main quantified impact measure was limited to recorded serious assaults in the larger Geelong police region. Data were collected from the year before the Accord to three years following. These showed an immediate fall from 117 serious assaults per 100,000 in 1988/89 to 73 in 1989/90—the year the Accord was introduced. Overall, the rate fell by 45% to 64 in 1992/93 (Felson et al., 1997, p. 128). In the same period, serious assaults per 100,000 rose 31% from an average of 77 to 101 for six comparative cities in Victoria. Despite fears that nightclub revenue would fall, police reported a '100 per cent increase in door takings at nightclubs' following the introduction of the Accord, 'and a 160 per cent increase in overall revenue' in the first 12 months (Felson et al., 1997, p. 126). Evidence regarding the positive effect of the Accord was also supported by qualitative data. According to Felson et al. (1997, p. 127):

> The police reported that young people were going home earlier and problems were far fewer. The crowds of intoxicated youths moving about the CBD were no longer evident in such numbers... The soft data indicate that

young people were still attracted to Geelong but apparently did not get in as much trouble while there.

The Accord evaluation team noted that the program was a classic example of problem-oriented policing, particularly through the 'analytic, problem-solving approach' (p. 129). Aspects of third-party policing and the enforcement pyramid were also evident in police pressure on licence holders. At the same time, the researchers noted that the process required a major shift in police attitudes and strategies: 'police, while not abandoning law enforcement, defined that traditional role as secondary and focused instead upon crime prevention' (p. 129). However, as in the Surfers Paradise example above, the Geelong program appears to have suffered from an eventual decay effect, with significant problems of alcohol-fuelled violence identified in the 2000s. A number of innovations were subsequently trialled but failed to show a positive effect (Miller et al., 2012a; see 'ID scanners and banned patron lists' above).

Newcastle: Lockouts and Closing Hours

In response to repeated public and police concerns about alcohol-related violence and property damage, the New South Wales Office of Liquor Gaming and Racing required 14 hotels in the city centre of Newcastle close by 3 am and refuse entry after 1 am (Kypri et al., 2011). However, a legal case required an adjustment to a 3.30 am closing time and 1.30 am lockout time. The lockout was referred to as a 'one-way door policy' (p. 304). In addition (p. 304),

> licensees were required to adopt a plan of management; were subject to compliance audits; had to have a dedicated responsible service of alcohol officer from 11 p.m. until closing; could not serve shots after 10 p.m.; had to cease selling alcohol 30 minutes prior to closing; could not permit stockpiling of drinks; had to adopt shared radio procedures; and all staff had to be notified of the conditions.

The program evaluation by Kypri et al. (2011) compared police-recorded non-domestic assaults in Newcastle, occurring between 10 pm and 6 am, pre- and post-intervention, with those in a nearby comparison site in Hamilton. Assaults declined by approximately 34% from 99.0 per quarter on average for 87 months pre-intervention (2001 to March

2007) to 67.7 per quarter for 18 months following the intervention. In Hamilton, the recorded assault rates were 23.4 and 25.5 respectively. Given the increase in the comparison location, the Newcastle restrictions were assumed to have reduced assaults by 37%. Overall, restrictions were projected to have prevented approximately 33 assaults per quarter. Assaults occurring between 3 and 6 am showed a 67% relative reduction in cases.

A follow-up study (Kypri et al., 2014), covering 3.5 years, identified a small increase in the assault rate in Newcastle. The average number of assaults per quarter in the second post-intervention period was 71—compared to 68 in the first post-intervention period and 99 in the pre-intervention period (p. 325). However, the final three quarters in the follow-up period showed low rates between 40 and 50. The results overall indicated that the original gains from the lockout program were largely sustained.

Of interest is the fact that the follow-up study included the introduction of a lockout system in the comparison area of Hamilton. From late August 2010, hotels were required to exclude new clients from 1 am on Saturdays and Sundays and to stop serving alcohol 30 minutes before closing. However, closing hours could be extended to 5 am. The results showed that there was only a small decline in the quarterly assault rate from 24 in the first post-intervention period to 22 in the second period (Kypri et al., 2014, p. 325). The researchers concluded that the differences between the Newcastle and Hamilton cases indicated the benefits of reduced closing times—from 5 am to 3.30 am in the Newcastle case—rather than lockouts on their own.

STockholm Prevents Alcohol and Drug Problems (STAD)

The 'STAD project' was initiated by the Stockholm County Council in 1996 in an effort to reduce intoxication and alcohol-related violence. The program was focused on the inner-city part of Stockholm and was based on (1) 'community mobilisation', (2) comprehensive training in Responsible Beverage Service (see above) and (3) 'stricter enforcement of existing alcohol laws' (Wallin et al., 2003, p. 271). Community mobilisation included establishment of an advisory group including the following (p. 272):

representatives from the Licensing Board, the Police Authority, the County Administration, the National Board of health, the organisation for restaurant owners, the trade union for restaurant staff, the Stockholm City Council, and influential restaurant owners from some of the most popular restaurants in Stockholm.

Advisory group meetings occurred up to five-to-six times a year. The mobilisation of the community primarily took the form of a communication strategy, with adverse reports from covert audits featured in the Media. Responsible Beverage Service training was made compulsory for licensed premises which stayed open past 1 am. The two-day training program covered a broad range of issues including relevant law, effects of alcohol, related drug problems and conflict management. Training covered approximately 50 venues. Enforcement included the issue of 'notification letters' by the Licensing Board in response to initial indicators of non-compliance. These notices gradually increased from 1997 to 2000. Audits of premises were conducted jointly by police and Licensing Board officers. However, surprisingly perhaps, 'the number of formal warnings and license withdrawals due to overserving ... has not increased since 1996' (p. 272), and the lack of detail about enforcement constitutes a major absence in the report.

Overall, the evaluation identified a 29% reduction in police-recorded violent crimes occurring between 10 pm and 6 am from four years before the intervention began to 2.5 years after. A control site showed a small increase in incidents. The audit data on the refusal of service of alcohol to intoxicated patrons showed an increase from 5% in the intervention area in 1996 to 55%, while the rate in the control area was 37%. A subsequent cost–benefit analysis focused on the licensed premises intervention for the period 1998 to September 2000, found that program costs of €796,000 were substantially exceeded by savings of €31.3 million—primarily covering health care and legal system costs (Mansdotter et al., 2007). It should be noted that it has been reported that efforts to replicate the success of STAD in other Swedish cities have been unsuccessful (VicHealth, 2012, p. 30). However, this is possibly because key features of STAD were already in place in these locations, whereas the STAD program was introduced in a laisse-faire environment with no responsible service of alcohol practices in place and police enforcement delivered on an ad hoc basis.

CONCLUSION

This chapter has shown that large reductions can be made in alcohol-related harms while allowing alcohol to remain part of leisure activities in entertainment settings. Minimising intoxication is a key overall goal, which is most likely to be achieved through a range of strategies that restrict easy access to alcohol or access while intoxicated. Not all individual strategies are well-attested on their own. A mix of strategies is most likely to be effective, especially in the area of enhanced guardianship, so that responsible authorities need to consider the relevance of a wide range of specific strategies when planning a crime and disorder reduction program. It appears that the best way to manage this is through the inclusion of all stakeholders, including through an ongoing management committee. Involvement of a permanent coordinator position is likely to be another highly beneficial strategy.

REFERENCES

Anderson, Z., Whelan, G., Hughes, K., & Bellis, M. (2009). *Evaluation of the Lancashire polycarbonate glass pilot project*. Lancashire Constabulary.

Babor, T. (2010). *Alcohol: No ordinary commodity - Research and public policy*. Oxford University Press.

Babor, T., Caetano, R., Casswell, S., Edwards, G., Giesbrecht, N., Graham, K., Grube, J., Grunewald, P., Hill, L., Holder, H., Homel, R., Osterberg, E., Rehm J., Room, R., & Rossow, I. (2003) *Alcohol: No ordinary commodity—Research and public policy*. Oxford University Press.

Berkley, J., & Thayer, R. (2000). Policing entertainment districts. *Policing: An International Journal of Police Strategies and Management, 23*(4), 466–491.

Campbell, C., Hahn, R., Elder, R., Brewer, R., Chattopadhyay, S., Fielding, J., Naimi, T., Toomey, T., Lawrence, B., Middleton, J., et al. (2009). The effectiveness of limiting alcohol outlet density as a means of reducing excessive alcohol consumption and alcohol-related harms. *American Journal of Preventative Medicine, 37*(6), 556–569.

Carr, K., & Spring, G. (1993). Public Transport Safety. *Crime Prevention Studies, 1*, 147–155.

Clarke, R. (2020). Assaults with glasses in bars and clubs in Lancashire, England. In M. Scott & R. Clarke (Eds.), *Problem-oriented policing: Successful case studies* (pp. 128–136). Routledge.

Curtis, A., Farmer, C., Harries, T., Mayshak, R., Coomber, K., Guadagno, B., & Miller, P. (2022). Do patron bans act as a deterrent to future anti-social offending? An analysis of banning and offending data from Victoria,

Australia. *Policing & Society, 32*(2), 234–247. https://doi.org/10.1080/104
39463.2021.1896516

Farmer, C., Miller, P., & Taylor, N. (2023). Do patron bans reduce crime? An examination of assault offences in Western Australia, before and after the introduction of police-imposed barring notices. *Policing and Society, 34*(4), 1–22.

Felson, M., Berends, R., Richardson, B., & Veno, A. (1997). Reducing pub hopping and related crime. *Crime Prevention Studies, 7*, 115–132.

Forsyth, A. (2008). Banning glassware from nightclubs in Glasgow (Scotland): Observed impacts, compliance and patron's views. *Alcohol and Alcoholism, 43*(1), 111–117.

Graham, K., & Homel, R. (2012). *Raising the bar: Preventing aggression in and around bars, pubs and clubs.* Routledge.

Graham, K., Osgood, D., Zibrowski, E., Purcell, J., Gliksman, L., Leonard, K., Pernanen, K., Saltz, R. F., & Toomey, T. (2004). The effect of the safer bars program on physical aggression in bars: Results of a randomized control trial. *Drug and Alcohol Review, 23*(1), 31–41.

Gruenewald, P., Freisthler, B., Remer, L., LaScala, E., & Treno, A. (2006). Ecological models of alcohol outlets and violent assaults: Crime potentials and geospatial analysis. *Addiction, 101*(5), 666–677.

Hauritz, M., Homel, R., Mcllwain, G., Burrows, T., & Townsley, M. (1998). Reducing violence in licensed venues: Community safety action projects. *Trends and Issues in Crime and Criminal Justice, 101*, 1–6.

Homel, R., Carvolth, R., Hauritz, M., McIlwain, G., & Teague, R. (2004). Making licensed venues safer for patrons: What environmental factors should be the focus of interventions? *Drug and Alcohol Review, 23*(1), 19–29.

Homel, R., Hauritz, M., Wortley, R., Mcllwain, G., & Carvolth, R. (1997). Preventing alcohol-related crime through community action: The surfers Paradise safety action project. *Crime Prevention Studies, 17*, 35–90.

Homel, R., Tomsen, S., & Thommeny, J. (1992). Public drinking and violence: Not just an alcohol problem. *The Journal of Drug Issues, 22*(3), 679–697.

Huckle, T., Parker, K., Mavoa, S., & Casswell, S. (2020). Reduction in late-night violence following the introduction of national New Zealand trading hour restrictions. *Alcohol Clinical Experience Research, 44*(3), 722–728.

Kypri, K., Jones, C., McElduff, P., & Barker, D. (2011). Effects of restricting pub closing times on night-time assaults in an Australian city. *Addiction, 106*(2), 303–310.

Kypri, K., McElduff, P., & Miller, P. (2014). Restrictions in pub closing times and lockouts in Newcastle, Australia five years on. *Drug and Alcohol Review, 33*(May), 323–326.

Liang, W., & Chikritzhs, T. (2011). Revealing the link between licensed outlets and violence: Counting venues versus measuring alcohol availability. *Drug and Alcohol Review, 30*(5), 524–535.

Lindsay, J. (2012). The gendered trouble with alcohol: Young people managing alcohol related violence. *International Journal of Drug Policy, 23*(3), 236–241.

Livingston, M. (2008). Outlet density and assault: A spatial analysis. *Addiction, 103*(4), 619–628.

Loxley, W., Toumbourou, J., Stockwell, T., Haines, B., Scott, K., Godfrey, C., Waters, E., & Patton, G. (2004). *The prevention of substance use, risk and harm in Australia: A review of the evidence.* Australian Government Department of Health and Ageing.

Macintyre, S., & Homel, R. (1997). Danger on the dance floor: A study of interior design, crowding and aggression in nightclubs. *Crime Prevention Studies, 7*, 91–113.

Mansdotter, A., Rydberg, M., Wallin, E., Lindholm, L., & Andreasson, S. (2007). A cost-effectiveness analysis of alcohol prevention targeting licensed premises. *European Journal of Public Health, 17*(6), 618–623.

McKnight, A., & Streff, F. (1994). The effect of enforcement upon service of alcohol to intoxicated patrons of bars and restaurants. *Accident Analysis and Prevention, 26*(1), 79–88.

Menéndez, P., Weatherburn, D., Kypri, K., & Fitzgerald, J. (2015). Lockouts and last drinks: The impact of the January 2014 liquor licence reforms on assaults in NSW, Australia. *Crime & Justice Bulletin: Contemporary Issues in Crime and Justice, 18*, 1–12.

Miller, P., Coomber, K., Ferris, J., Burn, M., Vakidis, T., Livingston, M., Droste, N., Taylor, N., Puljevic, C., De Andrade, D., Curtis, A., Grant, K., Moayeri, F., Carah, N., Jiang, J., Wood, B., Mayshak, R., Zahnow, R., Room, R., & Najman, J. (2019). *Queensland alcohol-related violence and night time economy monitoring (QUANTEM): Final report.* Deakin University.

Miller, P., Curtis, A., Millsteed, M., Harries, T., Nepal, S., Walker, S., Chikritzhs, T., & Coomber, K. (2021). Size does matter: An exploration of the relationship between licensed venue capacity and on-premise assaults. *Alcohol Clinical Experience Research, 45*(6), 1298–1303.

Miller, P., Diment, C., & Zinkiewicz, L. (2012a). The role of alcohol in crime and disorder. *Prevention Research Quarterly, 18*(August), 1–20.

Miller, P., Sønderlund, A., Coomber, K., Palmer, D., Tindall, J., Gillham, K., & Wiggers, J. (2012b). The effect of community interventions on alcohol-related assault in Geelong, Australia. *The Open Criminology Journal, 5*, 8–15.

Miller, P., Tindall, J., Sønderlund, A., Groombridge, D., Lecathelinais, C., Gillham, K., McFarlane, E., de Groot, F., Droste, N., Sawyer, A., Palmer,

D., Warren, I., & Wiggers, J. (2012c). *Dealing with alcohol-related harm and the night-time economy*. National Drug Law Enforcement Research Fund.
Nepal, S., Kypri, K., Pursey, K., Attia, J., Chikritzhs, T., & Miller, P. (2018). Effectiveness of lockouts in reducing alcohol-related harm: Systematic review. *Drug and Alcohol Review, 37*(4), 527–536.
Newbury-Birch, D., & Ferguson, J. (2023). *Alcohol, crime and public health*. Routledge.
Prenzler, T., Cairns, N., Moir, E., & Rayment-McHugh, S. (2022). *Nambour community safety review stage 1 report*. Sunshine Coast Council and University of the Sunshine Coast. https://research.usc.edu.au/esploro/outputs/rep ort/Nambour-Community-Safety-Review-Stage-1/99680498102621?instit ution=61USC_INST#file-0
Rossow, I., & Norstrom, T. (2012). The impact of small changes in bar closing hours on violence. The Norwegian experience from 18 cities. *Addiction, 107*(3), 530–537.
Stockwell, T. (2010). *Operator and regulatory best practices in the reduction of violence in and around licensed premises: A review of Australian and Canadian research*. Centre for Addictions Research of BC.
Streker, P. (2012). *Under the influence: What local governments can do to reduce drug and alcohol related harms in their communities*. Australian Drug Foundation.
Taylor, N., Coomber, K., Mayshak, R., Zahnow, R., Ferris, J., & Miller, P. (2019). The Impact of liquor restrictions on serious assaults across Queensland, Australia. *International Journal of Environmental Research and Public Health, 16*(22), 1–10.
Treno, A., Gruenewald, P., Lee, J., & Remer, L. (2007). The Sacramento neighborhood alcohol prevention project: Outcomes from a community prevention trial. *Journal of Studies on Alcohol and Drugs, 68*(2), 197–207.
VicHealth. (2012). *Pubs and clubs project: Literature review of different policy and community-based intervention and baseline trends of specific interventions in Geelong, Victoria (2000–2010)*. Victorian Health Promotion Foundation.
Victorian Community Council Against Violence. (1990). *Inquiry into violence in and around licensed premises*. Author.
Wallin, E., Norstrom, T., & Andréasson, S. (2003). Alcohol prevention targeting licensed premises: A study of effects on violence. *Journal of Studies on Alcohol, 64*(2), 270–278.
Wicki, M., & Gmel, G. (2011). Hospital admission rates for alcoholic intoxication after policy changes in the canton of Geneva, Switzerland. *Drug and Alcohol Dependence, 118*(2–3), 209–215.
Wiggers, J., Jauncey, M., Considine, R., Daly, J., Kingsland, M., Purss, K., Burrows, S., Nicholas, C., & Waites, R. (2004). Strategies and outcomes in

translating alcohol harm reduction research into practice: The Alcohol Linking Program. *Drug and Alcohol Review, 23*(September), 355–364.

Wilkinson, C., Livingston, M., & Room, R. (2016). Impacts of changes to trading hours of liquor licences on alcohol-related harm: A systematic review 2005–2015. *Public Health Research and Practice, 26*(4), 1–7.

CHAPTER 7

Safe Events: Festivals, Sports, Protests

Abstract Large gatherings are characteristic of free societies, but these events also create opportunities for criminal conduct and have the potential to make people feel unsafe. Effective safety strategies for events are likely to include careful planning and organisation, comprehensive risk assessments, entry screening, deterrence and de-escalation by security providers, and safe spaces. Formal partnerships between event organisers, police and private security also appear as a probable ingredient of success. Specifically, the democratic right to public demonstrations poses significant management issues for police and protest organisers. Too little control can result in rioting and extensive harms to property and persons. At the same time, in many places, responses to protests are characterised by police violence and denials of political rights. Police need to make use of best practice principles for managing demonstrations, focusing on negotiation and agreements with protest organisers, with shared responsibility for security.

Keywords Drugs · Sexual harassment · Negotiated management · Security management

T. Prenzler, *Preventing Crime and Disorder in Public Places*, Crime Prevention and Security Management,
https://doi.org/10.1007/978-3-031-63764-3_7

109

Background

Events like music festivals, concerts, markets, carnivals, parades and sporting competitions vary greatly in the extent to which standard security measures—such as guarding and access control—can be put into practice to protect all parties. Risk levels for crime will vary greatly but can be significant. Events frequently involve anonymous persons brought together in situations where unfamiliarity and crowding generate vulnerability. Drugs and alcohol can reduce inhibitions and natural defensiveness. Small numbers of predatory individuals and groups can hijack peaceful assemblies and create violence through provocation and peer pressure. Security might be a grudge expense for organisers trying to make money or it might be limited by open access criteria.

Events almost always represent a security challenge. Consequently, standard security management strategies of forecasting and pre-empting problems of crime and disorder need to be in place from the earliest point in the planning process (Draper et al., 2017). Optimal security management also includes comprehensive—or joined-up—coverage of all risks with opportunity-reducing measures and effective guardianship. Security roles for workers need to be clearly defined, with appropriate supervision and training. As much as possible, organisers should instal layered security, beginning with the outer perimeter of a venue and ensuring target hardening of high-value/high-risk inner locations. The use of a formal risk matrix is also of value in planning. The matrix plots the likely criticality, or harm, ensuing from an adverse event against the likelihood of the event occurring. For example, a terrorist attack or sexual assault might have a low probability of occurring but a high criticality, so prevention of these offences should be given a high priority. These principles can be made more effective through the use of situational, CPTED and problem-oriented policing strategies. Prominent examples include facilitating compliance, avoiding disputes, reducing frustration and stress, and enhancing informal and formal guardianship. The remainder of this chapter examines the application of these principles in ensuring safe activities at festivals, sporting competitions and protests.

FESTIVALS

Early on the morning of the 7th of October 2023, many of the 3,500 partygoers at the Supernova Music Festival in Israel, mainly young people, were still dancing when the site was attacked by heavily armed Hamas fighters from neighbouring Gaza. In a few seconds, the festival went 'from paradise to hell' (in Graham-Harrison & Kierszenbaum, 2023). The terror attack is most likely to have been opportunistic, as the Hamas fighters attempted a larger invasion of Israel. The death toll from the massacre at the festival has been put at approximately 260. There are documented cases of horrendous rapes. Forty hostages were taken and disappeared into Gaza. The festival was held 3.3 kilometres from the wall between Israel and Gaza. In hindsight, it was unwise for organisers to locate the event so close to a terrorist group committed to the annihilation of their country—although the high-tech border security system was reputed to be amongst the best in the world. The attacks, which included assaults on nearby villages, were considered a monumental failure of national defence intelligence, but one with direct consequences for safety at an innocent a-political music festival promoted as 'a journey of unity and love' (in Sherwood, 2023).

What this extreme case highlights is the need for security risk assessments which are wide-ranging and include worst-case scenarios. Most festivals and similar events will not face this level of risk, with dangers more commonly in the domain of assaults, sexual assaults, drug overdoses, thefts, fights, threats, litter and damage to property. A range of common security measures will help to reduce these problems. As we saw in regard to alcohol-related entertainment venues, reducing crowding can reduce provocations and also enhance natural surveillance. With that in mind, passageways and viewing areas need to be adequate to allow for easy movement and personal space. Festivals can also be alcohol-free or promote low-alcohol beverages and/or ensure responsible service of alcohol policies to minimise intoxication (see Chapter 6, Reducing Intoxication and Alcohol-related Crime in Entertainment Precincts). An adequate number of friendly security staff also needs to be on duty to deter misconduct and act effectively if security incidents occur. Good perimeter security, ticket checks and bag searches should also help to ensure attendance by legitimate users and exclude contraband such as weapons. Adequate signage, sight lines and the presence of storeholders and volunteer assistants can all assist with natural surveillance and informal guardianship.

Two areas of potential risk which are prominent in musical festivals are illicit drug use and sexual abuse. Preventive management strategies are discussed briefly in the following two subsections.

Drugs

Illicit drug use often goes hand-in-hand with music festivals as audiences seek to enhance the sensual and emotional experience of the music and camaraderie. Surveys have indicated that drug use can range between around half and two-thirds of festivals goers, and many take more than one type of drug—including ecstasy, marijuana and cocaine (Fileborn et al., 2019, p. 20). Zero tolerance was the traditional police approach to drugs at festivals, with officers seeking to deter and incapacitate offenders through seizures and arrests. Drug prohibition in many countries is based on medical advice about risks to health, although drug use at music festivals appears to carry very low risks of harm (Hughes et al., 2019, p. 7). Zero tolerance at festivals often involved intrusive body searches, either by hand or with sniffer dogs, which tended to be alienating and ineffective—fairly easily subverted through pre-entry consumption and on-site sales (Hughes et al., 2019). Some of these evasion strategies can lead to over-consumption and overdoses and avoidance of reporting overdose symptoms.

Official best practice policies in relation to drug possession and use at music festivals have gone through an evolutionary change in recent years away from law enforcement towards harm minimisation (Alcohol & Drug Foundation, 2019; Hughes et al., 2019). One practical example is free pill testing services, which allow persons with drugs to check the safety of the product they are carrying. Pill testing has been shown to be effective in identifying contaminants and moderating drug users' consumption (Alcohol & Drug Foundation, 2019, p. 5). Decriminalising possession of drugs for personal use can also reduce the harmful effects of criminalisation. Other strategies include on-site drug education programs and on-site medical services with rapid response capabilities. Encouragement of bystander intervention to call medical services will also likely reduce medical response times. 'Hydration stations' and 'chill out spaces' can also be beneficial. Festival staff, including security staff, also need to have first aid training, be trained in drug awareness and be ready to call for medical assistance when indicators suggest this is required.

Sexual Harassment and Assault

Sexual harassment and sexual assault at festivals are slowly being given attention as more incidents emerge and victims—mainly women—come forward (Fileborn et al., 2019). One survey in the United Kingdom found that '30% of young women and 14% of young men had experienced some form of sexual harassment or assault at a music festival' (Fileborn et al., 2019, p. 7). The most common forms of abuse were verbal harassment and 'unwelcome forceful dancing' (p. 7). An Australian study by Fileborn et al. (2019) involved observations conducted at the 2017–2018 Falls Festival, a survey of Festival patrons about their experiences at festivals generally, and interviews with 16 persons 'who had experienced, or had been involved in responding to, sexual violence at music festivals across Australia' (p. 3). On the positive side, the survey found that 61.5% of respondents 'usually' felt safe at festivals and 29% 'always' felt safe (total = 90.5%). At the same time, 95.1% believed that sexual harassment occurs and 88.6% believed that sexual assault occurs. The latter included 31.2% who felt that sexual harassment occurred 'often' and 30.2% 'very often'. The interviews indicated that sexual groping was common in dance and performance areas, the large majority of offenders were males and bystanders did not usually step in. In addition (Fileborn et al., 2019, pp. 4–5),

- Experiencing sexual violence of all kinds resulted in negative and often ongoing impacts, including hyper-vigilance, altered behaviour at festivals, anxiety and shock.
- Most participants did not report to police, security or festival staff. Those who did report typically recalled negative responses from authority figures, such as victim-blaming, not taking the report seriously and/or a failure to take appropriate action.
- Participants viewed the male-dominated nature of the music industry as a contributing factor to sexual violence in festival spaces.
- Zero tolerance policing of drugs and anti-social behaviour deterred participants from reporting to police.

As research about these problems increases so does available guidance on what is likely to work to reduce and prevent problems. For example, based on their multi-methods study above, Fileborn et al. (2019) developed the following practical set of summary recommendations (p. 5):

Festival policy and management:

1. Introduce clear protocols and consistent messaging about sexual violence, including consequences for perpetrators.
2. Increase the number of female police and security staff working on-site.
3. Develop multiple avenues for reporting sexual violence at festivals and ensuring all staff are adequately trained to receive and respond to these reports.
4. Implement processes for the systematic documentation of incidents of sexual violence.
5. Follow through on reports with feedback to victim-survivors.
6. Implement the provision of on-site access to appropriate support services.

Environment:

1. Provision of quiet 'chill out' spaces.
2. Ensure security and police are distributed throughout festival spaces, including regular patrols or emergency contact points on camping grounds.
3. Introduce section markers or signposting on camping grounds to improve way-finding.
4. Enhance lighting, particularly in isolated areas such as camping grounds.
5. Ensure signage establishing behavioural standards is clearly visible throughout all spaces at festival.
6. Introduce clear and consistently identifiable markers to note the location of security staff in and around performance spaces.

Cultural Change:

1. Continued efforts to make festival line-ups more gender equitable and diverse.

2. Encouragement of pro-social behaviour, such as bystander intervention.
3. Encouragement of an ethic of care amongst festival patrons.

In addition, consideration should also be given to security apps—now common on educational campuses. These are downloaded to mobile phones, with information on security services and quick call options for assistance (Barr, 2018).

SPORTS

Sporting events are also vulnerable to a range of violent and disruptive behaviours. These can be recurring and highly predictable, such as hooliganism and brawls between fans. In other cases, sporting events can quickly deteriorate into riots, arson and deadly stampedes. There is certainly no shortage of cases on the record. One example involving decades of controversy is that of the 1989 Hillsborough Disaster, in which 96 persons were crushed to death at a soccer match (Conn, 2016). Twenty-six parents of 56 children were killed. Thirty-seven teenagers were amongst the dead. A further 766 persons were injured. A major immediate causal factor was the opening of an exit gate in an effort to fix problems with delays at entry points to the stadium. An entry tunnel should have been closed when evidence of overcrowding was apparent. The start of the game should also have been delayed. The deaths and injuries were initially ruled as accidental, with fans alleged to be at fault. However, pressure from victims' families led to a second inquest which found that police and ambulance services were negligent in managing safety issues. The design of the stadium—with inadequate control of numbers in 'pens' that segregated fans—was also deemed to be a contributing factor.

Despite occurrences like these, there are numerous examples of good practice in the management of safety at sporting events. As with festivals, this involves the application of modern security management principles. The following two subsections provide examples of the successful management of safety at sports matches.

The FIFA World Cup in South Africa

In a book chapter titled 'Intriguing Paradox: The Inability to Keep South Africa Safe and the Successful Hosting of Mega Global Sporting Events', Bezuidenhout (2014) argued that the effective security strategies adopted by South African authorities in hosting international sporting events should be applied more broadly to mitigate the country's chronic problems of crime and disorder. According to the author, when it comes to 'mega events … it would appear that South Africa is the champion' (p. 222). Examples cited include the Rugby World Cup, FIFA Confederations Cup, African Cup of Nations, Indian Premier League Cricket and the FIFA World Cup. At the same time, 'South Africa cannot keep its citizens safe, has one of the highest murder rates in the world, and is notorious for violent strikes and police brutality' (p. 196). Policing is characterised by under-resourcing; inadequate leadership, management and training; tolerance for misconduct; and alienation between police and their communities.

According to Bezuidenhout (2014), the government adopted a standardised approach to security planning and management at these events, described in detail in the case of the 2010 FIFA World Cup. The Cup was said to be larger than the Olympic Games, with 450,000 visitors attending 64 matches over a month at ten stadiums in nine cities. Ticket sales reached 3.3 million. To obtain approval from FIFA to host the games, governments have to provide high-level security guarantees. In the South African case, a National Joint Operational and Intelligence Structure (Natjoints) took charge and established interconnected security protocols at every Cup location. The joined up approach began with a high security and clearance system at airport entry sites. Security then extended to Railway Police—with trains providing the main in-country transport for events—and beefed-up security on all transit routes, including security escorts for teams. Police numbers were increased at tourist centres, restaurants and other venues that attract fans. The police presence was described as 'visible but subtle, not to spoil the festive mood of the fans' (p. 210). The security web included police attention to black market tickets and counterfeit goods sales. Social welfare services were assigned to venues to assist lost children. Venue security included layered protection, with police prioritising perimeter security and private security playing a major role in interior perimeters. Non-uniformed officers and spotters were deployed in the crowds to deal quickly with unruly conduct. Multi-specialist Rapid Response Teams were on standby on a 24/7 basis to deal with major incidents. Anti-terror protocols included extensive use of surveillance technology. In anticipation of arrests, 56 special courts were established to deal expeditiously with cases. Court staff included interpreters and public defenders. Planning and budgeting included overtime payments and specialist crowd management training for police. Extensive use was made of mounted units. Professional conduct by police was reportedly a major area of focus. Police enlargements included 12 specialist police officers from the United Kingdom. International shared intelligence occurred in regard to soccer hooligans, with enforcement of bans applied at UK departure sites.

According to Bezuidenhout's (2014) account, this complex integrated security system operated without detracting from regular police services in South African communities. This was achieved in part through a boost to police numbers from a major recruitment drive prior to the Cup, as well as the deployment of a large reservist force. Approximately 10,000 voluntary part-time reservists were paid and fully engaged along with 31,000 police, with a further 10,000 reservists on standby (p. 211). Railway Police, fire officers, ambulance officers and other emergency services officers were on standby. Private security officer numbers were not reported. Volunteers were also involved.

One of the features of the Cup was the provision of 'fan parks', where audiences could watch games live for free on large screens. The main venue for this was the Grand Parade Fan Park in Cape Town. According to Nakueira and Berg (2014), these official parks, and similar public viewing areas, were a major success. Specifically (p. 66),

The host city embarked on a marketing campaign to promote these fan parks and the city of Cape Town made sure that it followed FIFA's Fan Park Event manual to construct the Grand Parade Fan Park. It is posited that the design, the staff that were deployed, and other arrangements made at the Fan Park were the main reasons that the fan park was a safe space in part by securing the site with 210 private security personnel. The main safety and security nodes such as SAPS (South African Police Service), Traffic, Disaster and Risk management, Fire and Rescue, Metro Police and Law Enforcement were deployed in and around the fan park all with varying roles, which contributed to securing the fan park. These roles were articulated in the FIFA 2010 Grand Parade Fan Park Emergency and Contingency Plan. Additionally, the Venue Operation Control Centres had representatives from each department that were deployed including Event Management and Event Security. All public viewing areas were expected to follow the same design and were to be implemented as mandated by the Host City Agreement and the FIFA Fan Park Manual irrespective of whether or not they were official fan parks.

Security at the 2010 World Cup was considered a major success, fostering 'a sense of pride, confidence, optimism and belief' amongst government, police and security officials (Bezuidenhout, 2014, p. 216). More generally (p. 216),

> [The World Cup] remains a great feat for a country whose ability to host an event of this magnitude was repeatedly under scrutiny by the global community. Many fans expressed their fears to come to the crime-invested country like SA. However, after the tournament many fans hailed SA and indicated that they would like to return to the warm and friendly rainbow nation. Even FIFA was impressed and paid the government significant bonuses for the successful hosting of the event.

It was also reported that general crime rates declined in the areas where security operations occurred. At the same, there appeared to be no lasting impact on policing strategies, and crime returned to normal levels. This is despite the fact that South Africa's successful 'public safety recipe' could be applied on a permanent society-wide basis to make South Africa a safer place (Bezuidenhout, 2014, p. 209).

Security at the Melbourne Cricket Ground

Sarre (2014) and Sarre and Prenzler (2011) reported on an observational study of the working relationship between public police and private security at the Melbourne Cricket Ground. The governing body, the Melbourne Cricket Ground, had 14 full-time in-house security staff. A security firm, MSS, supplied security officers for events. Victoria Police supplied paid volunteer officers who worked over-time. The overall security program was managed through a partnership agreement between police, MSS and the Melbourne Cricket Club. The power to restrict entry and remove persons was a key security mechanism. The *Major Sporting Events Act 2009 (Vic)* includes the following authority: 'an event organiser … is responsible for, and has all powers necessary to control access to, an event venue or an event area by participants, officials, volunteers, spectators and other persons during an operational arrangements period for that event' (in Sarre & Prenzler, 2011, p. 78).

Observers were present at the security coordination box and during a briefing for security personnel during an Australian Football League (AFL) match. The briefing highlighted several security risks for attention, including 'lost children, … smuggled in alcohol, and drunken and obnoxious behaviour' (Sarre & Prenzler, 2011, p. 88). The venue hosts several different sporting codes, and the researchers noted that 'the different demographics between cricket, football, and soccer crowds mean that different security arrangements are required for each sporting event', using a 'risk level matrix' (p. 88). Specifically, 'certain combinations of AFL teams attract more potential trouble than others' (p. 88). Determining the best ratio of police to security officers was a key process. In the case of the event under observation, there were 20 police and 125 MSS officers, a ratio of around 1:6.25. Sarre (2014) noted that 'the number of police needed for most events is declining, as risks at most events are becoming fewer and fewer' (p. 108). This was attributed in part to the bag searches at stadium entrances that ensure bottles and alcohol do not enter the venue. Despite this a-symmetry, in terms of the operating relationships between the two groups, police were in charge. They were also responsible for sending in officers to manage more disruptive behaviour (p. 108):

> In the MCG stadium, MSS staff outnumbered police but the police took the lead role in dispatching officers to deal with unruly patrons. MSS staff were the first responders (in charge of breaches of conditions of entry such as being in possession of contraband) while police were responsible for breaches of the criminal law. Police are empowered by legislation to apply 'on-the-spot' penalty notices and 24-hour banning notices, and to take photos of offenders.

At the same time, 'Police are specifically directed to backup the decisions made by security personnel. Indeed, VicPol management encourage security personnel to report any police officer who does not support the decisions of security personnel' (Sarre, 2014, p.108).

Overall, security was deemed to be highly effective on the occasion under observation, although the crowd also appeared to be acting responsibly. 'At the end of the night, all of the stakeholders gathered for a de-briefing. Apart from a couple of evictions and some patrons caught with contraband, it was a relatively event free night' (Sarre & Prenzler, 2011, p. 89). The study also found that the main advantage of contracting private security was the lower costs compared to police. Police charged the Cricket Club around twice the fees charged by MSS. At the same time, stadium ground staff reported that the greater authority and visual deterrent effect of uniformed police was necessary to ensure the effectiveness of the police/security mix.

SAFE PROTESTS

The right to express a political opinion through participation in a public demonstration is considered a fundamental human right and is an essential feature of legitimate democratic government (UNHRC, 2020). Mass protests, sometimes supported by police, have also driven many cases of progressive reform. According to Baker (2016, p. 58):

> Protest has been a dynamic and vibrant force behind much fundamental democratic change in the Western world. Labour movement, suffragette, land rights, human rights, independence movements, anti-apartheid, anti-war, environmental and numerous diverse protests have achieved remarkable advances, often against considerable opposing forces... Police have been present at many defining moments in history; the dynamics of police interaction with protesters can be significant in determining the legitimacy of protest behaviour.

It is little wonder then that a primary strategy by which autocracies obtain and retain power is to brutally suppress public demonstrations. A good test of the depth of democracy, and the legitimacy of government, is the extent to which a jurisdiction not just allows, but facilitates, protests in public places. Nonetheless, police in a democracy are faced with the classic dilemma of how to support legitimate group-based expressions of opinion while also protecting lives and property and allowing people to go about their normal business (Baker, 2016).

Protests can very quickly turn into destructive riots. One of the most famous cases on record is the 1992 Los Angeles Riots. Four police officers charged over the systematic assault of African-American man Rodney King were acquitted by what many thought was a biased mainly-white jury. Protests turned into riots which lasted for three days across the city. Arson and vandalism were estimated to have cost US$1 billion at the time.

Thousands of injuries were reported and at least 53 deaths (Prenzler, 2021, pp. 57–58). In 2011, protests broke out in England after police shot dead Michael Duggan. Over five nights, cities and towns across England 'were engulfed by fire and violence' (Mohdin & Murray, 2021). The riots reportedly started after Duggan's family, making enquiries about his death, were turned away from a police station. It has been estimated that 15,000 people participated and there were 4,000 arrests; five people were killed, and £200 million worth of property was damaged including at 3,800 shops.

These two examples of protests that turned into riots involved alleged triggers from controversial police actions. Racial conflict, poverty, inequality and associated anger were also contributing factors. At the macro-level, these circumstances point to the need for good relations between police and their communities within the framework of a broader social contract that creates genuine opportunities for shared prosperity and wellbeing. In addition, at the micro-level, police tactics are often crucial in how a demonstration plays out: 'Police responses to a protest event can either inflame or diffuse a potentially violent situation' (Baker, 2016, p. 69). In that regard, Baker describes a number of dilemmas that police face in managing protests (p. 57):

> Tactically, should police remove perceived ringleaders and troublemakers prior to or during a protest? Will such action incite or calm a crowd? Should police treat all protest groups in the same manner or differentiate between causes and individuals? Do police tactics facilitate the majority of protesters to cooperate with police or do they alienate the majority towards more radical and extremist elements? Should police enforce summary offences relating to obstruction or allow street protest to proceed?

Peaceful protests are often undermined by ideological extremists and/ or criminals who want to engage in violence and attack police as their enemies. This is a key consideration for management. In addressing the challenge of supporting peaceful protest, a clear best practice set of principles and strategies has emerged. In practice, even the best plans are not foolproof, but it is incumbent on the police, and associated government authorities, to follow the playbook as far as possible. According to Redekop and Pare (2010), approximately 90% of protests in democracies that recognise the right to protest occur without disorderly conduct (p. 134). This is in part a product of the application of democratic policing principles, especially the 'negotiated management' approach (below), but it also means that contingencies against violence will often not need to be activated.

Best Practice Planning and Support

It is easy to think of good practice in police tactics as something that develops flexibly in response to the actions of protestors. However, best practice entails processes that are in place well before the day of the demonstration. Organised adaptability is one of these. The following list of principles is developed from research on the successful and unsuccessful management of protests by police (e.g., Baker, 2016; Gillham & Noakes, 2007; Hall & de Lint, 2004; HMIC, 2011; Reicher, 2011; Waddington, 2007).

- *The right to protest* needs to be enshrined in legislation. Authorisation should be available for marches that require street closures or other likely disruptions to normal activities. Legislation should oblige police to support peaceful protests and diverse expressions of interest as much as possible. Police use-of-force should be minimal and applied as a last resort to protect life and property.
- *A place to protest* needs to be available. Protestors want maximum attendance, maximum media attention for their cause, and a direct line of communication with politicians and policymakers. The ideal method usually involves marching, with chants and banners; followed by a gathering where speeches are made. This can be facilitated by the creation of (1) a marshalling area, (2) a marching path, such as a major road closed to traffic or an open mall area and (3) a terminus with a large open space for the whole group to gather and hear speeches. Ideally, the terminus will be in front of a democratic capital building. The latter can also allow for delegates to enter the parliament and present their claims and/or a petition to government leaders. Inadequate access and exposure can provoke violence.
- *Detailed planning* is fundamental, and should include the widest number of variables and contingencies to ensure protest management is as capable, adaptable and effective as possible.
- *Intelligence* is also essential for effective planning. In particular, police need to be informed of the identities and purposes of

protestors, including factions and conflicts, without intruding on their civil liberties through unwarranted covert surveillance.

- *Negotiated management* involves protest organisers and police meeting in advance of events and coming to agreements about event times, march routes, road closures, and acceptable and unacceptable conduct. This includes organisers being fully informed of their legal rights and responsibilities and penalties for infractions. Police positions need to be reliable and clearly understood. Negotiated management should include post-event debriefs.

- *Self-policing* or *co-production of security* involves protest organisers messaging participants about conduct standards and appointing crowd marshals to reinforce safety messages and step in to de-escalate conflict.

- *Facilitating compliance* involves police and authorities ensuring protest organisers are informed of their legal obligations and police conscientiously attempting to accommodate organisers' preferences. As we have seen with other public order issues, organisers and government regulators need to think about people's basic needs for food and water, toilet stops, respite zones and transport in order to reduce frustration and stress. Ambulance services need to be on hand.

- *Less-lethal weaponry* are police tools that can be incapacitating without killing or seriously harming the target. Examples include tear gas, pepper spray, tasers and water cannons. However, these can all be misused, so that standards and training need to be consistently applied (OHCHR, 2020).

- *Target hardening* might be necessary in some cases and needs to be considered and organised in advance. This can include protecting high-value and vulnerable buildings with sand bagging, barriers, boarded-up windows and doors, and the presence of police guards or security officers.

- *Removing troublemakers* is a tactic that can easily backfire and provoke violence. However, it is often deemed essential to sort legitimate from illegitimate protestors, especially where the latter are intent on inflaming violence.

- *Contingency readiness* or *backup* refers to the availability of extra resources if event management and de-escalation fail and violence break outs. This can involve having specialist police tactical teams located nearby, fire and ambulance services and even military forces in high-risk situations.

- *Thorough up-to-date training* of police at all levels of the organisation is essential to ensure protest management represents best practice.
- *Police independence* is necessary to prevent party-political and ideological bias. Applications for march permits (to police or a justice department) need to be decided on objective criteria related to civil liberties and public safety.
- *Accountability* means that the actions of all parties can be scrutinised through mechanisms such as objective complaints systems and access to information. Strategic use of video, including body cameras, can assist with any subsequent legal issues.
- *Removing targets* is a situational measure that might be applicable in cases such as large gatherings of international representatives in city centres. These conferences of high-polluting states, many involved in human rights violations, with unresolved legacies of colonial abuses, simply invite mass protests that create chaos in central business districts. These meetings could be held just as productively—if they ever achieve much for ordinary people—in remote resorts where access by protestors is easily prevented or more easily managed.

CONCLUSION

Planning and comprehensive management are universally seen as the best ways to ensure safe and happy festivals, concerts, sporting events, demonstrations and other large public gatherings. This involves the application of standard security management techniques with clearly assigned responsibilities, environmental scans, and pre-emption of opportunities and provocations for violence, but without a heavy-handed and intimidating policing presence. The ability to protest and express an opinion in public, including through mass gatherings, should be considered a fundamental human right which police are obligated to support within the context of peacefulness.

REFERENCES

Alcohol and Drug Foundation. (2019). *What is harm reduction and why is it important at music venues and events?* https://cdn.adf.org.au/media/doc uments/ADF_StayingSafeAtEvents.pdf

Baker, D. (2016). Policing contemporary protest. In T. Prenzler (Ed.), *Policing and security in practice: Challenges and achievements* (pp. 56–73). Palgrave-Macmillan.

Barr, L. (2018, September 3). For safety on campuses, law enforcement increasingly turns to apps. *ABC News.* https://abcnews.go.com/US/safety-cam puses-law-enforcement-increasingly-turns-apps/story?id=57558628

Bezuidenhout, C. (2014). Intriguing paradox: The inability to keep South Africa safe and the successful hosting of mega global sporting events. In J. Albrecht, M. Dow, D. Plecas, & D. Das (Eds.), *Policing major events: Perspectives from around the world* (pp. 195–224). CRC Press.

Conn, D. (2016, April 27). Hillsborough inquests jury rules 96 victims were unlawfully killed. *The Guardian.* https://www.theguardian.com/uk-news/2016/apr/26/hillsborough-inquests-jury-says-96-victims-were-unlawfully-killed

Draper, R., Ritchie, J., & Prenzler, T. (2017). Principles of security management. In T. Prenzler (Ed.), *Understanding crime prevention: The case study approach* (pp. 137–150). Australian Academic Press.

Fileborn, B., Wadds, P., & Tomsen, S. (2019). *Safety, sexual harassment and assault at Australian music festivals: Final report.* https://doi.org/10.13140/RG.2.2.30091.85280

Gillham, P., & Noakes, J. (2007). More than a march in a circle: Transgressive protests and the limits of negotiated management. *Mobilization: An International Quarterly, 12*(4), 341–357.

Graham-Harrison, E., & Kierszenbaum, Q. (2023, October 13). Supernova massacre. *The Guardian.* https://www.theguardian.com/world/2023/oct/12/supernova-massacre-israeli-soldiers-patrol-the-site-as-survivors-tell-their-stories

Hall, A., & de Lint, W. (2004). Making the pickets responsible: Policing labour at a distance in Windsor, Ontario. In S. Nancoo (Ed.), *Contemporary issues in Canadian policing* (pp. 337–375). Canadian Educators Press.

HMIC. (2011). *Policing public order.* Her Majesty's Inspectorate of Constabulary. https://s3-eu-west-2.amazonaws.com/assets-hmicfrs.justicein spectorates.gov.uk/uploads/policing-public-order-20110208.pdf

Hughes, C., Barratt, M., Ferris, J., & Winstock, A. (2019). *Australian music festival attendees: A national overview of demographics, drug use patterns, policing experiences and help-seeking behaviour.* National Drug and Alcohol

Research Centre. https://ndarc.med.unsw.edu.au/sites/default/files/ndarc/resources/DPMP%20Bulletin%2028%20-%20Profiles%20and%20policing%20of%20Australian%20music%20festival%20attendees.pdf

Mohdin, A., & Murray, J. (2021, July 30). 'The Mark Duggan case was a catalyst': The 2011 England riots 10 years on. *The Guardian.* https://www.theguardian.com/uk-news/2021/jul/30/2011-uk-riots-mark-duggan

Nakueira, S., & Berg, J. (2014). Innovations in the governance of security: Lessons from the 2010 world cup in South Africa. In J. Albrecht, M. Dow, D. Plecas, & D. Das (Eds.), *Policing major events: Perspectives from around the world* (pp. 59–73). CRC Press.

OHCHR. (2020). *Guidance on less-lethal weapons in law enforcement.* Office of the United Nations High Commissioner for Human Rights (OHCHR). https://www.ohchr.org/sites/default/files/Documents/HRBodies/CCPR/LLW_Guidance.pdf

Prenzler, T. (2021). *Ethics and accountability in criminal justice.* Australian Academic Press.

Redekop, V., & Pare, S. (2010). *Beyond control: A mutual respect approach to protest crowd-police relations.* Bloomsbury Academic.

Reicher, S. (2011). From crisis to opportunity: New crowd psychology and public order policing principles. In T. Madensen & J. Knutsson (Eds.), *Preventing crowd violence* (pp. 7–23). Lynne Rienner.

Sarre, R. (2014). Policing major events in Australia: A private security model of police cooperation. In J. Albrecht, M. Dow, D. Plecas & D. Das (Eds,), *Policing major events: Perspectives from around the world* (pp. 105–114). CRC Press.

Sarre, R., & Prenzler, T. (2011). *Private security and public interest: Exploring private security trends and directions for reform in the new era of plural policing.* University of South Australia & Australian Research Council.

Sherwood, H. (2023, October 9). How the Hamas attack on the Supernova festival in Israel unfolded. *The Guardian.* https://www.theguardian.com/world/2023/oct/09/how-the-hamas-attack-on-the-supernova-festival-in-israel-unfolded

UNHRC. (2020). *General comment No. 37 (2020) on the right of peaceful assembly (article 21).* United Nations Human Rights Committee. https://documents-dds-ny.un.org/doc/UNDOC/GEN/G20/232/15/PDF/G2023215.pdf?OpenElement

Waddington, D. (2007). *Policing public disorder: Theory and practice.* Willan.

CHAPTER 8

Public Toilets Matter!

Abstract This chapter analyses an issue of major importance to all users of public spaces. Toilets with public access are commonly characterised by experiences that are unpleasant and insecure. The standard of facilities represents an excellent test of the quality of democratic governance, and this often-neglected area of place management requires a revolution in design and political commitment. In this policy domain, access, amenity, hygiene, privacy and safety constitute enmeshed categories. CPTED again provides a set of highly applicable techniques in combination with wider standards applied to comfort stops. Visibility, image, natural surveillance, guardianship, target hardening, entry control and assisting compliance all have direct relevance for a safe and happy toilet experience in a public location.

Keywords Guardianship · Natural surveillance · Amenity · Gender neutral facilities

© The Author(s), under exclusive license to Springer Nature Switzerland AG 2024
T. Prenzler, *Preventing Crime and Disorder in Public Places*, Crime Prevention and Security Management,
https://doi.org/10.1007/978-3-031-63764-3_8

127

PUBLIC TOILETS: PROBLEMS AND ISSUES

Public toilets meet a basic human physical need, they help prevent the problem of public urination (Clarke, 1997, p. 25), and they support standards in public health and public order. In regard to public urination, they provide a potentially highly effective alternative to police arrests and prosecutions, and they also prevent an expensive and unpleasant clean-up process. In the language of situational prevention, they assist compliance and remove excuses. Overall, it would seem obvious that public toilets should be numerous, easily accessible, super clean, comfortable and very safe.

However, it appears that there is a universal problem with public toilets failing to meet the most basic standards, let alone optimal standards. Citing a variety of sources, Corradi et al. (2020) state that 'emotions, fears and thoughts about the use of public bathrooms have been associated with the use of a very intimate place without the usual control and safety offered by the home environment' and that 'using public toilets is, generally, a negative experience with relevant psychological repercussions' (p. 1). These include anxiety, stress and frustration. At the same time, avoiding toilets altogether can also have adverse physical health effects, including pain and the aggravation of chronic conditions.

Subsets of the population with a variety of health issues are highly dependent on convenient access to toilets. Corradi et al. report that between six and eight million people globally suffer from inflammatory bowel diseases and require quick and easy access to public toilets (2020, p. 2). Wheelchair users and other mobility impaired persons are a large group who require modifications to standard toilet designs.

Women also have higher needs than men for privacy, security and amenity and so are more likely to be negatively impacted by inadequate services (Corradi, et al., 2020). Transgender users of toilets are another group typically unrecognised by traditional designers. Transgender persons can face highly stressful dilemmas over which binary-based facility to use and can also be vilified over their choices (Martin & Brourd, 2023). Research in the United States found that 43% of transgender students avoided school toilets because they felt uncomfortable or unsafe (Kosciw et al., 2018, p. 15).

Public urination is a specific crime issue, often concentrated in entertainment districts. Berkley and Thayer's (2000) survey of police managers with jurisdiction over entertainment areas included a question about public urination. Eighty-two per cent stated that public urination was a problem (p. 471). For 52%, it was 'always' or 'frequently' a problem. Entertainment areas are particularly prone to this offending behaviour because 'large volumes of alcohol are consumed, nightclubs and bars often have inadequate restroom capacity, and cities have provided no public restrooms' (p. 469).

However, provision of toilets in public spaces can bring another set of problems. A degree of privacy and seclusion make them attractive locations for crimes against the person, including assaults, sexual assaults, theft and robbery (Berkley & Thayer, 2000). Stalking and loitering can also be concentrated in and around public toilets. They are often attractive locations for property crimes such as vandalism and graffiti. Public toilets are also notorious as places for sexual hook-ups. This is generally recognised as an unacceptable form of behaviour in a public place that often includes unwanted solicitations. Nonetheless, traditional arrest policies seem to do considerable harm to perpetrators' lives with little evidence of a reduction in activity (Desroches, 1991, p. 16). The partial privacy offered by toilets also make them attractive for drug dealing and drug consumption.

Lack of fit between people's needs and available comfort stations curtails people's ability to use and enjoy public spaces. Adverse effects range from mild to severe, with direct consequences for equality, freedom and wellbeing. Public toilet provision and design have failed to keep pace with positive modern trends in areas such as more walking and cycling, more use of public transport, outdoor recreation, pandemic prevention, social inclusion and carbon neutrality (PHLUSH, 2015). As Berkley and Thayer state, 'an absence of public restrooms conveys the message that the city lacks courtesy and hospitality' (2000, p. 469). The lack of safe places for a comfort stop also conveys the message that authorities don't care about the security of citizens and visitors.

SETTING STANDARDS

Addressing the challenges associated with public restrooms begins with identifying best practice standards. Here, again, it is productive to combine CPTED and situational crime prevention techniques with more welfare- and wellbeing-oriented principles. The following subsections provide a range of readily applicable design standards for toilets that should be adopted as a comprehensive package to maximise the safe and happy use of public spaces.

Availability

To be effective, both inside and outside venues, toilets need to be visible and accessible, with adequate supply to prevent queuing. Local authorities often try to leave it to businesses to supply facilities. There is a rationale for a legal requirement for shopping centres and larger cafes and restaurants to provide facilities. However, public access is often limited in these settings, and opening hours and cleanliness are very much at the discretion of the owners. Lack of public facilities can create a nuisance problem for shopkeepers and make for an annoying process for customers to obtain keys. Therefore, it is incumbent on democratic authorities to take responsibility and ensure supply in all the locations where people congregate and are likely to require access. Clear signposting is essential and opening times also need to be clearly signed and set across a sufficient span of hours to meet demand. As an intermediate measure, some local authorities pay commercial facilities to provide public access to their toilets, with signage to that effect (PHLUSH, 2015, p. 18)—although full public provision across the desired span of hours represents best practice.

Construction and maintenance costs appear as a major deterrent to the adequate provision of public restrooms. This does, however, represent a lack of vision. In theory, public toilets are a good investment for authorities who wish to attract members of the public who will spend money in the area and contribute to tax revenues. Public toilets can in fact be income generators, in part by providing convenient locations for nearby food carts, markets and entertainment (PHLUSH, 2015). Alternative funding sources include advertising and donations (PHLUSH, 2015). Advertising can even be placed on toilet paper. Costs can be defrayed if volunteers adopt a public toilet and contribute to maintenance. Product dispensers for condoms, sanitary products and nappies can also provide some income (Hertfordshire Constabulary Crime Prevention Design Service & The British Toilet Association, 2010, p. 49). Numerous smart design features, described in the following subsections, entail reduced cleaning and repair costs. Pre-fabricated modular designs should reduce the costs associated with new builds, replacements and upgrades.

'Street urinals', 'urilifts' and 'pop-ups' represent attempted solutions to shortages of public toilets, especially for specific high-demand times associated with night-time entertainment precincts (Hertfordshire Constabulary Crime Prevention Design Service & The British Toilet Association,

2010, p. 45). These are typically male urinals and often have very limited privacy. Public visibility makes them undesirable, and the costs involved with the mechanics would suggest permanent unisex facilities would be much better.

Improving public toilet availability might be limited in many locations by the lack of available spaces. However, some creativity might be helpful here. For example, disused buildings can be modified or areas under bridges and stairways can provide convenient locations (PHLUSH, 2015, p. 16).

Location and Guardianship

Consistent with CPTED theory, public toilets need to be situated in ways that optimise visibility. This involves a counter-intuitive step. The natural tendency is to hide toilets away because of the 'yuk' factor and the fact that people are embarrassed being seen entering and leaving a toilet. However, from a crime prevention perspective, visibility is a key first step in building a secure environment. Potential offenders will be deterred if they are conscious of being observed by nearby persons who can intervene directly or call authorities. Natural surveillance can be enhanced by locating toilets within sight of cafes, train stations, bus stops, taxi ranks, shops, libraries and cinemas. The availability and visibility of restrooms are also likely to attract legitimate users who will enlarge the population of informal guardians. Office buildings with windows that look down on a toilet block can also aid natural surveillance. Ideal locations will be within sight of formal guardians by way of police stations or security desks, or concierge or information desks (Crowe, 1991, p. 123). Security patrols should ensure they include public toilets on their beats. Isolated locations should be avoided wherever possible, although this is of course often unavoidable to ensure access in more remote locations such as national parks. Cameras can provide proxy surveillance, but to be effective they should be linked to monitoring stations with radio contact to rapid response providers. Camera systems should include two-way communication, and the presence of cameras should be clearly signposted.

A variety of design features will enhance natural surveillance and reduce hiding places and entrapment points. In that regard, entrances need to be clear of clutter and as open as possible. The temptation to build privacy screens across the entrances to direct entry facilities (see below) needs to be resisted. Designs that create alleyways and corridors leading to restrooms should also be fiercely resisted. Landscaping should be used to add to the attractiveness of a location while ensuring sightlines are not compromised. Lighting should also enhance the attractiveness and useability of a facility without creating shadows that can serve as hiding places and add to the fear of crime (Hertfordshire Constabulary Crime Prevention Design Service & The British Toilet Association, 2010, p. 21). It is probably best to turn lights off when facilities are closed, although keeping sensor lights on can help deter potential offenders.

Public toilets are often standalone buildings, which makes sense in many cases, but this can allow for hiding places at the sides and the rear of buildings. Incorporating facilities into a larger building, such as a kiosk or restaurant or parks office, can reduce this problem. Seating areas adjacent to facilities can be beneficial for persons waiting on other persons using a toilet. Seats should be near enough to encourage natural surveillance while deterring loitering (Hertfordshire Constabulary Crime Prevention Design Service & The British Toilet Association, 2010, p. 15). Persistent loitering, including for sexual purposes, can be dealt with by police or security officers as trespass and subject to cautions and banning orders (Desroches, 1991).

Target Hardening

A variety of target hardening measures can be used to prevent vandalism and forced entry. Obvious features include sturdy fittings (such as lights), cladding, and night gates and locks. Placing toilets within larger buildings can eliminate the chances of a break-in from the sides or rear. Ducted plumbing removes hiding places for drugs, weapons and other contraband, and also makes cleaning easier (PHLUSH, 2015, p. 34). Paper dispensers should be lockable to prevent theft. Any cleaning or other maintenance equipment stored on-site also needs to be locked up in a secure receptacle. Doors, hinges and locks on stalls need to be sufficiently robust to deter attacks, but they should include locks that can be opened with rescue tools and should be sufficiently weak so they can be broken in an emergency when tools can't be accessed. Some designs have doors opening outwards to prevent a collapsed person blocking a door. This can, however, create a hazard with doors hitting patrons. One solution is to have the cubicles sufficiently deep so that there is space for both the door to open inward and a person to be prone on the ground at the seat end (see direct entry toilets below). Another security mechanism is a 'viewing out only facility', or 'peephole', which can allow users to check the outside area before exiting (Hertfordshire Constabulary Crime Prevention Design Service & The British Toilet Association, 2010, p. 28).

Amenity and Hygiene

The CPTED concept of image tells us that signs of neglect send a message that legitimate authorities are not fully in charge, contributing to feelings of insecurity (Chapter 2). There is a likely direct correlation therefore between the quality of public toilets and users' feelings of being protected. In that regard, toilets need to be clean, which means they need to be cleaned frequently. In these post-COVID-19 days of heightened concern about hygiene, all facilities should have soap dispensers, a means of drying hands, and hand sanitiser. User-operated non-touch flush mechanisms and non-touch water dispensers improve hygiene and reduce vandalism breakage points. Electric hand dryers reduce the need for paper towelling—which can facilitate littering and even arson (Hertfordshire Constabulary Crime Prevention Design Service & The British Toilet Association, 2010, p. 32). A mirror allows people to check their appearance and deal with any issues. Small conveniences like mirrors, shelves and hooks reinforce the message that the relevant authorities care and that the user's safety is therefore likely to matter as well. (Hooks need to be weak enough to stop their use as suicide hanging points.) Bins for sanitary products should also be included. Hinged seats aid hygiene but should not have lids so users can check the contents before deciding on going further. Overall, most toilets should be more spacious to ensure sufficient personal space and reduce the sense of entrapment likely in an enclosed space.

Attractive facilities will attract legitimate users and contribute to an improved social environment. Some toilets can even have features that put them on the map and draw in tourists, such as the beachside 'Loo with a View' in Australia (Sunshine Coast News, 2022). The overall design of some public toilets has been so unique and appealing that they have been described as 'public art' (Miller, 2023, p. 7). Cycle parking and dog tethering points are additional conveniences.

Access and Equity

The background section of this chapter briefly outlined a variety of disabilities that require additional access features. A number of innovations in this area are now increasingly common. For example, wheelchair-access toilets have more space, raised seats and grab rails. They also benefit people who are frail or on crutches. However, these stalls are often located within the traditional male/female row stalls. In this situation, they still require some navigation and potential close encounters with other persons. They also exclude caregivers, especially caregivers of a different sex. Consequently, disability access toilets, or 'all abilities' toilets, should be standalone units, either outside male/female facilities or as part of a set of direct access stalls (more on these below). 'Changing Places' toilets add a further layer of access for more severe disabilities, with features such as extra space, a hoist and an automatic door, amongst other things (Changing Places, 2023). Space for caregivers also adds a layer of guardianship. Call buttons and adult-size change tables can also be useful. Disability carparks should be located as close as possible to facilities.

Privacy, Personal Space and Safety

When it comes to public toilet design, adequate privacy, personal space and safety are requirements that have a particularly close affinity and overlapping functionality. One example of a deficit in this area is the traditional cubicle—or stall—design, with large gaps between the floors and the walls. Who wants to look at their neighbour's feet and possibly have to deal with unwanted solicitations through this space (Reuters, 2009)? Stalls also often have a vertical gap between the door and the walls that can provide a view inside (Reuters, 2009). Cubicles usually lack ceilings, and walls are often so low that a person can stand on a seat and look into the neighbouring cubicle. This traditional and almost ubiquitous structure uses fewer materials and makes cleaning easier, but it also creates far too much proximity and noise and too many opportunities for harassment. Ideally, there should be no gaps between the walls and floor, the doors and walls, and between the doors and the floor. Walls and doors should reach high enough to prevent voyeurism while allowing for airflow. When it comes to cleaning, if the right waterproof materials are used then low areas and floors can still be easily hosed out and mopped dry. Where row stall formats are retained, male trough urinals should be replaced with individual urinals with privacy screens, including low-set urinals for boys.

Common areas in public toilets should be sufficiently spacious to prevent congestion and allow people to keep a safe distance from others. In row toilets, washbasins should be located well away from urinals and stalls. Pathways and common areas outside toilets should be broad enough to prevent congestion and allow people to keep a safe distance (Hertfordshire Constabulary Crime Prevention Design Service & The British Toilet Association, 2010, p. 12).

Some useful work on improved safety in common areas in row-style toilets has been done by CPTED specialist Tim Crowe (1991, p. 132). He describes a less safe layout with a single entrance through a hinged door into the semi-private area: a layout that contributes to making people feel that they can be easily trapped inside and attacked. A safer design incorporates entrances without doors, with a privacy wall ensuring the inside area cannot be viewed from the outside. Ideally, there will be two open entrance ways, partially to prevent people bumping into each other and partly to increase the number of escape routes.

Attendants

Attendants have been employed in some locations to provide access control and collect fees. Attendants can be effective in ensuring safe spaces, especially for women and other more vulnerable groups (Korbynn et al., 2018). The cost of this approach may be lessened or removed through the use of volunteer organisations, particularly for larger events, or through levies imposed on night-time entertainment businesses. In general, paying to enter a toilet should be avoided as it reduces access; although in some cases fee-paying luxury toilets can provide subsidies for nearby free toilets (PHLUSH, 2015, p. 22).

Maintenance, Quality Audits and Surveys

Apart from inadequate cleaning, another common problem with public toilets is lack of restocking of materials and repair of broken fixtures. Public toilets often lack sufficient toilet paper, run out of soap and have broken locks. Other defects include doors that don't close properly, broken seats, and taps that spray water. Apart from setting up frequent cleaning schedules, authorities need to organise frequent auditing of facilities and clear lines of responsibility for restocking and repairs to ensure defects are immediately fixed and shortages are immediately rectified. Seats that can be easily replaced will aid maintenance. Regular audits involving systematic physical inspections and stakeholder consultation are also a good idea. Signs with websites, e-mail addresses and phone numbers for public maintenance notifications are also strongly recommended.

Public surveys of the type developed by Corradi et al., (2020, see above), should also be utilised on a regular basis. The authors' Public Bathroom Perception Scale utilises 14 scaled items across three categories: 'privacy, ease of use and cleanliness' (p. 3). Safety issues receive some indirect attention in the privacy category but should be a separate explicit category in a comprehensive questionnaire. Ease of finding and accessing toilets could also be more explicit. PHLUSH (2015) provides a wider range of categories that can be incorporated into a questionnaire, including safety topics.

More generally, as noted above in relation to graffiti, cleaners should provide daily reports on maintenance requirements and any crime and safety issues they observe. There is also no substitute for frequent regular independent audits covering all aspects of toilet amenity and safety with findings reported on local authority public websites to enhance accountability and spur remedial action.

Gender-Neutral Facilities and Direct Entry Stalls

When it comes to the needs and interests of women—as a group vulnerable to male predation—privacy and safety have traditionally been provided by segregated facilities. In recent years, this practice has been challenged by the needs of transgender, or non-binary, persons who find themselves excluded from the traditional male/female options. Confusion in this area has been recognised as a safety issue, as summarised in the following set of questions by Martin and Brourd (2023, p. 1):

> The public bathroom has become a lightning rod for a general social anxiety about safety and gender. Are women safe if a trans woman uses the same bathroom? What does it mean to the gender (and indeed sexuality) of men if a trans man uses the 'men's bathroom'? Aren't children at risk if anyone can "decide" they are trans and walk into a public bathroom?

While these questions are indicative of the concerns of some heterosexual persons, the authors argue that it is in fact non-binary persons who are probably most at risk of aggression and violence in these situations.

There are several ways to manage this issue. One is to allow and encourage general access to disabled and/or parents' toilets. However, it could be argued that this still normalises binary distinctions and also does not clearly resolve the issue—as a fairly wide discretion still applies for users. A better option is to make all toilets gender-neutral—or 'unisex' or 'gender-inclusive'—with direct entry to stalls (Martin & Broard, 2023; PHLUSH, 2015). In other words, the traditional setup with row stalls within a larger semi-private room should be done away with. This change has the added likely advantages of making more stalls available to women, obviating the privacy problem associated with male urinals, and making it easier for parents to take young children of the opposite sex into a toilet and for caregivers to assist disabled persons (PHLUSH, 2015). Children who might be considered old enough to go to the toilet on their own are also separated from potential offenders.

At the same time, the layout of gender-neutral toilets does mean that predatory persons have an excuse for being in the vicinity. Consequently, external visibility and guardianship are particularly important in this context, as is attracting legitimate users with activity generators such as food outlets, playgrounds and markets. Gender-neutral toilets in schools have been cited as a major means of reducing opportunities for bullying (Francis et al., 2022). They should also deter sexual activities if there is sufficient visibility and natural guardianship (Desroches, 1991).

Gender-neutral toilets can also provide some efficiencies by having common wash stations. External washup areas are also likely to deter theft of soap and vandalism of hardware. Including urinals in stalls can also speed up turnover and stop males urinating on seats (Washroom Essentials, 2023). Adequately resourced facilities would include toilet seats, urinals, change tables and disability access in all stalls. Direct entry stalls also mean that cleaning can take place one stall at a time without the need to close whole sections.

Graffiti Prevention

Stopping graffiti on public toilets should be easy. One approach is to trial graffiti resistant paints and surfaces (Hertfordshire Constabulary Crime Prevention Design Service & The British Toilet Association, 2010,

p. 20). These 'reduce rewards' when tags smear, but they can still require cleaning. It's best to find an alternative if possible, and probably the best way to do this is to operationalise the CPTED principle that bare surfaces attract graffiti. From that perspective, incorporating facilities into a larger building can remove three external walls. Another simple and attractive fix for graffiti on external walls is the use of vines (growing vertically) or creepers (growing horizontally). The right lattice or other support needs to be used so the frames don't provide access to the roof. Some pruning is required but this should be easy as a small part of a larger maintenance and beautification program for public spaces. If this approach is not viable for some reason, then rapid removal is one of the better known means of minimising graffiti (see Chapter 5 on transport systems). With this in mind, frequent audits and reporting by cleaners and users can facilitate rapid repair, reducing rewards and deterring offenders.

'Legitimate street art' is another viable deterrent to graffitists, which also enhances location aesthetics (Waingiwriter's Blog, 2012). This takes the form of commissioned murals and other types of graphic work which are applied to surfaces. Some local governments will pay professional artists to paint walls in common areas, and these works can become tourist attractions and attract legitimate users. In other cases, school groups and other community groups are likely to be willing to undertake public art projects for free. Art can also be used on the internal walls. The use and retention of stencils can allow for rapid repair.

Sustainability

Environmental sustainability is an additional modern criterion that should be added to access, amenity, hygiene, privacy and safety. Public toilets are often located in open areas where their roof spaces can be used for solar panels. Windy areas can be linked to wind generators. Including batteries means that the facilities can operate outside daylight hours. This is especially important when going off-grid in cases where there are disability features dependent on electricity, such as automatic doors. Water tanks and passive temperature moderation systems—such as ventilation ports and thicker walls—can also assist with net-zero carbon targets. Recycled materials can be used in construction. Water usage can be reduced with dual flush buttons and waterless urinals. Skylights reduce electricity costs and improve visibility and ambience.

Other Design-Against-Crime Innovations

Several miscellaneous crime prevention innovations should be mentioned here for consideration in improving public toilets and reducing crime. Of interest is an innovation that makes use of high-tech glass walls. Tokyo has reportedly seen the introduction of transparent public toilets. The walls allow potential users to see into empty stalls to be sure they are clean and that they are not occupied by potential assailants (Kelleher, 2020). When the door is locked the walls turn opaque. Blue lights are sometimes used inside toilets because they make veins hard to see and reportedly stop users of intravenous drugs from self-injecting (Miller, 2023, p. 8). Some locations have attempted to prevent public urination with a product described as 'the paint that pees back', which repels liquids and reportedly splashes urine back on the shoes and trousers of offenders (Winkless, 2016).

Conclusion

The quality of public toilets is fundamental to people's enjoyment of public spaces and the livability of towns and cities. Consequently, high-functioning and super-safe public toilets should be considered a basic human right, high on the agenda of local authorities and town planning specialists. The fact that this is not the case in most locations speaks to the quality of democracy and the substandard performance of politicians and public servants. Building and maintaining quality public restrooms is easy. Excuses should not be accepted. It's a highly worthwhile investment, and designers and operators should incorporate principles of CPTED to enhance safety while also making use of the many best practice guides available to optimise amenity and privacy. We need a 'toilet revolution' that will fix all the problems associated with inadequate and substandard provision, including safety issues (Miller, 2023, p. 3).

References

Berkley, J., & Thayer, R. (2000). Policing entertainment districts. *Policing: An International Journal of Police Strategies and Management*, 23(4), 466–491.

Changing Places. (2023). *Why changing places?* https://changingplaces.org.au/

Clarke, R. (1997). Introduction. In R. Clarke (Ed.), *Situational crime prevention: Successful case studies* (pp. 2–43). Harrow and Heston.

Corradi, G., Garcia-Garzon, E., & Barrada, J. (2020). The development of a public bathroom perception scale. *International Journal of Environmental Research and Public Health, 17*(21), 1–14. https://doi.org/10.3390/ijerph 17217817. PMID:33114539;PMCID:PMC7662958.

Crowe, T. (1991). *Crime prevention through environmental design: Applications of architectural design and space management concepts.* Butterworth-Heinemann.

Desroches, F. (1991). Tearoom trade: A law enforcement problem. *Canadian Journal of Criminology, 33*(January), 1–21.

Francis, J., Sachan, P., Waters, Z., Trapp, G., Pearce, N., Burns, S., Lin, A., & Cross, D. (2022). Gender-neutral toilets: A qualitative exploration of inclusive school environments for sexuality and gender diverse youth in Western Australia. *International Journal of Environmental Research and Public Health, 19*(16), 1–13. https://doi.org/10.3390/ijerph191610089

Hertfordshire Constabulary Crime Prevention Design Service and The British Toilet Association. (2010). *Publicly available toilets problem reduction guide.* http://www.btaloos.co.uk/wp-content/uploads/2014/01/PubliclyA vailableToiletsProblemReductionGuide.pdf

Kelleher, S. (2020, August 16). *Why Tokyo's new transparent public restrooms are a stroke of genius.* https://www.forbes.com/sites/suzannerowankelleher/ 2020/08/16/why-tokyos-new-transparent-public-restrooms-are-a-stroke-of-genius/

Korbynn, M., Bennett, S., Maxwell, C., Ling, J., James, K., Bell, E., Trachsel, H., Rausch, R., Liew, N., & Li, Y. (2018). *Solving public urination: The open washroom program.* https://citystudiovancouver.com/wp-content/uploads/ 2018/04/Public-Washroom-Program-REPORT.pdf

Kosciw J., Greytak, E., Zongrone, A., Clark, C., & Truong, N. (2018). *The 2017 National School Climate Survey: The experiences of lesbian, gay, bisexual, transgender, and queer youth in our nation's schools.* Gilsen. https://www.glsen.org/sites/default/files/2019-10/GLSEN-2017-National-School-Climate-Survey-NSCS-Full-Report.pdf

Martin, J., & Brourd P. (2023, June 2021). Bathrooms are political: How gender-inclusive toilets can combat indignity and violence. *The Conversation.* https://theconversation.com/bathrooms-are-political-how-gender-inc lusive-toilets-can-combat-indignity-and-violence-207447

Miller, J. (2023, March 22). *Why are public restrooms still so rare?* https://ame ricanrestroom.org/wp-content/uploads/2023/04/Why-Are-Public-Restro oms-Still-So-Rare-The-New-York-Times-3-22-23.pdf

PHLUSH. (2015). *Public toilet advocacy toolkit.* https://toolkit.phlush.org/phl ush-toolkit-download/

Reuters. (2009, January 9). *Ex-Senator Craig accepts sex sting guilty plea.* https://www.reuters.com/article/us-usa-politics-craig/ex-senator-craig-accepts-sex-sting-guilty-plea-idUSTRE5075L720090108/

Sunshine Coast News. (2022, September 28). *Have your say: Concept plans revealed for Mooloolaba's Loo with a View precinct.* https://www.sunshinecoas tnews.com.au/2022/09/28/your-choice-two-plans-revealed-for-loo-with-a-view-parkland/

Waingiwriter's Blog. (2012, September 4). *What is legitimate street art?* https://wangiwriter.wordpress.com/2012/09/04/636

Washroom Essentials. (2023). *Planning a unisex bathroom: The pros, cons & practicalities.* https://www.washwareessentials.co.uk/content/unisex-bathroom

Winkless, L. (2016, July 31). *The science behind 'the paint that pees back'.* https://www.forbes.com/sites/lauriewinkless/2016/07/31/the-science-behind-the-paint-that-pees-back/?sh=51924e1a701b

CHAPTER 9

It's a Process: Best Practice in Preventing Crime and Disorder in Public Places

Abstract This final shorter chapter focuses on the design and implementation side of crime prevention programs. A major theme of the book is that a wide variety of strategies can be deployed to make large reductions in crime and disorder, and to improve people's feelings of security and their peaceful use of public spaces. A key issue, however, is how to select and manage those strategies most likely to be effective. To do this, a best practice process model of crime prevention has emerged, primarily generated from the many successful case studies on the record—and, to some extent, from the unsuccessful cases. Primary features of this methodology include comprehensive diagnostics, consultation, committee management, appointment of a project manager, full implementation, evaluation, modification and maintenance. Incorporating the interests of marginalised groups—ensuring inclusion and supporting diversity—should also be a fundamental consideration.

Keywords Four stage model · Management Committee · Program manager · Evaluation

© The Author(s), under exclusive license to Springer Nature Switzerland AG 2024
T. Prenzler, *Preventing Crime and Disorder in Public Places*, Crime Prevention and Security Management,
https://doi.org/10.1007/978-3-031-63764-3_9

CRIME PREVENTION PROCESS MODELS

The case studies reported in the book frequently included a description of process aspects of the intervention; that is, how individuals or groups organised, implemented and managed the project. 'Project' is a common word, although it tends to imply a temporary action. 'Program'—implying something ongoing—is perhaps a better term. Regardless, studies of successful crime reduction interventions have led to a variety of process models most likely to generate ongoing success. We saw several of these in Chapter 2. These included the four steps in the SARA model, situated within problem-oriented policing (POP): 'Scan, Analyse, Respond, Assess' (Eck & Spelman, 1987; see also Kennedy, 2020). Clarke described a similar five step process for situational prevention (1997, p. 15):

1. Collection of data about the nature and dimensions of the specific crime problem;
2. Analysis of the situational conditions that permit or facilitate the commission of the crime in question;
3. Systematic study of possible means of blocking opportunities for these particular crimes, including analysis of costs;
4. Implementation of the most promising, feasible and economic measures;
5. Monitoring of results and dissemination of experience.

Clarke and Eck's (2003) booklet *Become a Problem-Solving Crime Analyst in 55 Small Steps* provides a more nuanced set of actions.

There are also many useful guides that include standards around ethics, community consultation, social inclusiveness, observance of human rights and democratic accountability (e.g., Marks et al., 2005; Mazerolle & Prenzler, 2004; Trojanowicz & Bucqueroux, 1990; White et al., 1996). In addition to these, there are guides available for higher level support from governments to generate crime prevention programs (e.g., Australian Institute of Criminology, 2012; UNODC, 2010). Government-facilitated demonstration projects can be an important way of showcasing success and encouraging similar projects. Government funding, including start-up grants, can also be an important mechanism for getting programs off the ground.

A Four-Stage Model

The following provides a convenient numbered list of what might be considered essential steps and criteria for a successful program to prevent crime and disorder in public places. This was developed from the guides referenced above and the case studies discussed in the book. The points are intended to provide guidance but also to serve as a checklist for programs designers and program personnel to ensure all major issues are addressed.

Stage 1: Development

1.1. Establish a development committee.

  1.1.2. Ensure stakeholder representation.

1.2. Define the problems.

  1.2.1. Specify all aspects of the problems that need to be fixed.

  1.2.2. Use multiple sources of data such as police-recorded crime, security incident reports, cleaning and maintenance reports, public opinion and experience surveys, and focus groups.

  1.2.3. Use these sources as baseline data for the impact evaluation (below). Try to include data that go back some years before the intervention.

1.3. Diagnose the problems.

  1.3.1. Specify all possible causal aspects of the problems.
    1.3.1.1. Identify offender motives and tactics.
    1.3.1.2. Identify victim vulnerabilities.
    1.3.1.3. Identify situational variables that facilitate and inhibit crime.
    1.3.1.4. Use data above at 1.2.2. and additional data if possible, e.g. offender interviews.

  1.3.2. Consult the scientific literature on what has and hasn't worked in reducing this crime problem. Consider strategies that appear most relevant to your site.

1.4. Design interventions.

  1.4.1. Develop a detailed set of tailor-made interventions most likely to be effective.

1.4.2. Ensure that issues of procedural justice are addressed; e.g., does the draft plan include overly draconian and punitive measures that need to be moderated or removed?

1.4.3. Ensure that issues of social justice are addressed; e.g., are the needs and interests of minority and marginalised groups addressed?

1.4.4. Ensure stakeholder input. One means to do this is through an inclusive management committee (above 1.1.). Consider public forums and media outreach.

1.4.5. Include a budget.

1.4.6. Seek adequate funding. Consider diverse sources of funding.

Stage 2: Implementation

2.1. Turn the development committee into an ongoing management committee.

2.2. Appoint a program manager whose sole task is to manage the intervention program.

2.3. Activate all elements of the plan (1.4.1.)

Stage 3: Evaluation

3.1. Process evaluation.

3.1.1. Use diverse sources to identify how well the program was developed and implemented; e.g., was consultation adequate; are resources adequate?

3.1.2. Use multiple measures, including interviews with program personnel, stakeholders and partners.

3.2. Impact evaluation.

3.2.1. Adopt a pre- and post-intervention format for data.

3.2.2. Include at least one comparison site if possible.

3.2.3. Include as many valid measures as possible, consistent with point 1.2.2 above.

3.2.4. Include perceptions of crime and feelings of safety.

3.2.5. Look for possible displacement or diffusion of benefits.

3.2.6. Share the results in a transparent open access format.

Stage 4: Follow-up

4.1. Maintain interventions that appear effective and fair.
4.2. Introduce modifications to improve impacts if possible as part of a commitment to continuous improvement.
4.3. Ensure resources and infrastructure are in place to sustain the program.
4.4. Use the process evaluation results to make improvements to program management.
4.5. Schedule routine follow-up evaluations.
4.6. Consider replication programs that can spread the benefits and also further test what works or doesn't work at the level of transferability.
4.7. Use experiences to lobby relevant authorities for macro-level changes that will assist micro-level actions.

Specific Elements and Issues

Management and Personnel

Not all public space crime prevention programs will need a management committee and program manager, but these elements certainly represent best practices where it's feasible to include them. Committees allow for different talents and interests to be combined to optimise the chances of success. Scheduling regular meetings ensures that the program remains under scrutiny and doesn't fall into neglect. A strong independent chairperson is needed to ensure that the committee is not co-opted by dominant persons or narrow sectional interests. (A spirit of cooperation and compromise is not always in full force.)

Employing a full-time or part-time program manager—or 'project officer'—should significantly boost the chances of success by ensuring there is at least one person with dedicated responsibility for moving the program forward. The person needs to have a good knowledge of crime prevention methods and an ability to work with a diverse array of stakeholders. The report by Homel et al. (1997) on the Surfers Paradise Safety Action Project includes useful material on the work of the project officer—as a key force in the initial success of the intervention in reducing alcohol-related violence. The following comments on the officer's female gender are worth noting (pp. 79–80):

> A ... somewhat unexpected, conclusion of the project was that the gender of the Project Officer was a crucial factor in gaining licensees' confidence and commitment. The reality in Australia is that the majority of licensees are male and the 'drinking culture' is driven by male values and standards, with an emphasis on control and dominance within drinking environments. Practices that encourage excessive drinking and aberrant behaviour are encouraged and often seen as a rite of passage for young men entering adulthood. In this context, it seems that the female Project Officer was not perceived as posing a challenge or a threat to the male licensees, and was less likely than a man to encounter resistance when attempting to persuade licensees to adopt more responsible alcohol policies.

Evaluation Issues

Crime prevention programs are beset by evaluation problems and issues. There is a democratic obligation for program managers to report the impacts of the interventions they introduced, along with process evaluation results that include social justice and other management accountability issues. However, the number of variables affecting crime and disorder in a particular location, and the difficulty of accurately measuring them, makes evaluation challenging. Nonetheless, at a minimum, there should be a genuine effort to capture as many indicators as possible from before and after the intervention and also across the intervention site and a comparison site. This is necessary to identify as many outcomes as possible and to try to separate the influences of the interventions from other possible influences. Comparison sites are a normal part of this evaluation process, and they can also help identify possible displacement or diffusion of benefits.

Social scientists and stakeholders will vary in the standards they apply to evaluation. Some will require strict scientific standards, including a matched control site and tests for statistical significance (Bates et al., 2017, pp. 8–9; for more information see the Maryland Scientific Methods Scale Farrington, 2003). Others will accept less exacting criteria for assessing impacts and deciding whether or not the interventions were the main influences on the recorded changes and whether or not the program has been successful. For example, sometimes it is not possible to adopt a suitable comparison site, so that a 'within-group' assessment is the only option (e.g., Homel et al., 1997). Nonetheless, in such cases, an environmental scan should be used to attempt to identify possible influences on the program outcomes beyond the interventions. Some useful guides in that regard include Blatter and Haverland's 'process tracing' approach (2014) and Pawson and Tilley's (2004) concept of 'realist evaluation'.

One of the more problematic aspects of evaluation concerns the effects associated with multiple prevention strategies. Did just one of the interventions cause the observed changes and the others are redundant? If more than one intervention had an impact, what were the proportional effects? In some cases, different data sources might indicate variable effects. For example, interviews with offenders might indicate that lighting was a strong deterrent. In other cases, surveys of the users of spaces might identify the visibility of uniformed patrol officers as the main driver of improved feelings of safety. However, in many cases, it is likely that the separate influences of different interventions cannot be teased out and that ambiguity has to be tolerated. And it seems that multiple interventions are often essential to cover the range of possible causal factors in crime and disorder. 'It's a package', was a phrase used by one of the architects of the famous Gainesville Convenience Store Robbery Reduction Program (in In the Line of Duty, n.d.). Implied in this phrase is the view that all elements of the program were essential, and worked together, perhaps synergistically, for success. In this case, there were eight primary interventions mandated by legislation and associated with an 80% reduction in offences (In the Line of Duty, n.d.; see also Clifton, 1987):

1. Removal of all visual obstructions [to allow a clear view from the outside to the inside],
2. Equal candlepower [lighting] outside as there is inside [to remove hiding places],
3. Train the clerks [usually involving compliance to prevent injuries],
4. $50 or less in the cash register [to reduce rewards],
5. Drop safe [to hold the cash above $50],
6. Time-release safe [to limit access to cash for change],
7. Two clerks on the scene [at high-risk times between 8 pm and 4am] and
8. Surveillance cameras in full view.

Maintenance

Maintenance of programs involves a major challenge. One of the programs referenced repeatedly in this book—the Surfers Paradise Safety Action Project—decayed when the project coordinator position ended. According to the longer-term report, venue management put profits over safety in promoting liquor consumption (Homel et al., 1997). In addition, the government liquor licensing authority—the regulator—failed to enforce standards. Similar processes are also apparent in some other case studies. In addition, case study evaluations also often suffer from a lack of follow-up reporting on ongoing impacts and issues. One possible solution for this is a permanent program manager position, with a liaison role between all parties, as well as the establishment of a permanent management committee and public reporting requirements.

Partnerships

Finally, mention should be made of the importance of partnerships in crime prevention. A great many of the successful case studies reported on in this book involved some kind of collaboration between interested parties. A key concept here is 'buy-in', which refers to the perception of a likely benefit from cooperating and making a contribution within an individual's or agency's capacity (Prenzler & Mihinjac, 2017, p. 132). The three main categories of groups likely to be involved in partnerships are democratic governments, the private sector (commercial interests) and community sector (voluntary groups and charities). Partnerships can also occur within these groups. Small voluntary changes by parties, such as reducing clutter in a shop window or reporting observed misconduct, can be of assistance. Financial contributions, as we saw with Business Improvement Districts, can allow for the employment of specialist service providers such as program manager, patrol officers and maintenance teams. Wellbeing and welfare issues, especially those concerning disadvantaged groups, are also most likely to be effectively addressed if relevant agencies are included in planning and management. Inclusive planning and management committees are a key means of optimising this aspect of crime prevention programs.

In terms of policies and actions that facilitate partnerships, the United Nations has published several useful guides (e.g., UNODC, 2010). United Nations support is based in part on the idea of increasing equality in security. The report *Civilian Private Security Services: Their Role, Oversight and Contribution to Crime Prevention and Community Safety* (UNODC, 2011) recommends that governments create specialist bodies to implement programs, along with investments in research and training. The United Nations guidelines also emphasise the importance of effective licensing systems to ensure adequate competency and integrity amongst private security industry partners. As indicated above, protocols also need to be in place to prevent conflicts of interest and ensure that procedural justice and social justice principles are foregrounded. One review of factors involved in crime prevention partnerships identified the following ingredients likely to lead to successful outcomes (Prenzler & Sarre, 2016, 163):

- a common interest in reducing a specific crime or crime set,
- effective leadership, with personnel with authority from each partner organisation driving participation,
- mutual respect,
- information sharing based on high levels of trust in confidentiality,
- formal means of consultation and communication, such as committees, forums and e-mail networks,
- willingness to experiment and consider all ideas,
- formal contractual relationships are not always essential,
- additional legal powers are not always necessary on the security side,
- data-rich projects appear more likely to generate effective interventions and demonstrate success.

CONCLUSION

The research evidence canvassed in this book is strongly supportive of likely success in the mission to reduce crime and disorder in public spaces. This is a crucial task for democratic authorities and all responsible place managers, with a great deal at stake in terms of people's safety, security and wellbeing. Special efforts to achieve these goals are absolutely essential, but they can be managed well or poorly. To ensure the best chances of success, responsible authorities should follow a step-by-step process which involves consultative site-specific diagnostics, development of a fully informed intervention plan, implementation through a representative management committee, with ongoing evaluation and a continuous improvement process. A variety of frameworks should be used to inform this systematic problem-solving process, including situational crime prevention, crime prevention through environmental design (CPTED), problem-oriented policing, procedural justice, social justice and the social contract. Other useful concepts include place management, community policing, third-party policing, reassurance policing, broken windows theory and quality-of-life policing. These approaches all involve proactive methods of predicting and pre-empting offending, rather than simply responding to crime and disorder events as they occur. When looking at place management, local governments need to take a leadership role—in initiating projects, coordinating participants and leveraging resources. In addition, crime prevention program design must avoid discrimination and exclusion, and support diversity and inclusion.

References

Australian Institute of Criminology. (2012). *National crime prevention framework*. https://www.aic.gov.au/sites/default/files/2020-05/national-crime-prevention-framework.pdf

Bates, L., Belsham, D., & Miles-Johnson, T. (2017). Crime prevention: Setting standards. In T. Prenzler (Ed.), *Understanding crime prevention: The case study approach* (pp. 1–12). Australian Academic Press.

Blatter, J., & Haverland, M. (2014). Case studies and (causal-) process tracing. In I. Engeli & C. Rothmayr Allison (Eds.), *Comparative policy studies* (pp. 59–84). Palgrave Macmillan.

Clarke, R. (1997). Introduction. In R. Clarke (Ed.), *Situational crime prevention: Successful case studies* (pp. 1–43). Harrow and Heston.

Clarke, R., & Eck, J. (2003). *Become a problem-solving crime analyst in 55 small steps*. https://popcenter.asu.edu/sites/default/files/55stepsuk_0_0.pdf

Clifton, W., Jr. (1987). *Convenience store robberies in Gainesville, Florida: An intervention strategy by the Gainesville Police Department*. Gainesville Police Department.

Eck, J., & Spelman, W. (1987). *Problem-solving: Problem-oriented policing in Newport News*. United States National Institute of Justice.

Farrington, D. (2003). Methodological quality standards for evaluation research. *The Annals of the American Academy of Political and Social Science, 587*(1), 49–68.

Homel, R., Hauritz, M., Wortley, R., McIlwain, G., & Carvolth, R. (1997). Preventing alcohol-related crime through community action: The Surfers Paradise Safety Action Project. *Crime Prevention Studies, 17*, 35–90.

In the Line of Duty. (n.d.). *Convenience store robbery decline* [video]. https:// lineofduty.com/product/v02p03/

Kennedy, D. (2020). Problem-oriented public safety. In. M. Scott & R. Clarke (Eds.), *Problem-oriented policing, successful case studies* (pp. 281–296). Routledge.

Marks, E., Meyer, A., & Linssen, R. (2005) *Beccaria-Standards for ensuring quality in crime prevention projects*. Council for Crime Prevention of Lower Saxony. https://beccaria.de/Kriminalpraevention/en/Documents/beccaria_quality%20in%20crime%20prevention.pdf

Mazerolle, L., & Prenzler, T. (2004). Third party policing: Considering the ethical challenges. In M. Hickman, A. Piquero, & J. Greene (Eds.), *Police integrity and ethics* (pp. 163–187). Wadsworth.

Pawson, R., & Tilley, N. (2004). Realistic evaluation. In S. Matthieson (Ed.), *Encyclopaedia of evaluation* (pp. 362–367). SAGE.

Prenzler, T., & Mihinjac, M. (2017). Reducing violence and disorder: Seven case studies. In T. Prenzler (Ed.), *Understanding crime prevention: The Case study approach* (pp. 121–136). Australian Academic Press.

Prenzler, T., & Sarre, R. (2016). Public-private crime prevention partnerships. In T. Prenzler (Ed.), *Policing and security in practice: Challenges and achievements* (pp. 149–167). Palgrave-Macmillan.

Trojanowicz, R., & Bucqueroux, B. (1990). *Community policing: A contemporary perspective*. Anderson.

UNODC. (2010*). Handbook on the United Nations crime prevention guidelines: Making them work*. United Nations Office on Drugs and Crime. https://www.unodc.org/pdf/criminal_justice/Handbook_on_Crime_Prevention_Guidelines_-_Making_them_work.pdf

UNODC. (2011). *Civilian private security services: Their role, oversight and contribution to crime prevention and community safety*. United Nations Office on Drugs and Crime. https://www.unodc.org/documents/justice-and-pri son-reform/Expert-group-meeting-Bangkok/IEGMCivilianPrivateSecurity/UNODC_CCPCJ_EG.5_2011_1_English.pdf

White, R., Murray, G., & Robbins, N. (1996). *Negotiating youth-specific public space: A guide for youth and community workers, town planners and local councils*. Youth Programs Unit, Department of Training and Education Co-ordination, Government of New South Wales.

INDEX

© The Editor(s) (if applicable) and The Author(s), under exclusive license to Springer Nature Switzerland AG 2024
T. Prenzler, *Preventing Crime and Disorder in Public Places*, Crime Prevention and Security Management,
https://doi.org/10.1007/978-3-031-63764-3

GPSR Compliance

The European Union's (EU) General Product Safety Regulation (GPSR) is a set of rules that requires consumer products to be safe and our obligations to ensure this.

If you have any concerns about our products, you can contact us on ProductSafety@springernature.com

In case Publisher is established outside the EU, the EU authorized representative is:

Springer Nature Customer Service Center GmbH
Europaplatz 3
69115 Heidelberg, Germany

The manufacturer's authorised representative in the EU is Springer
Nature Customer Service Centre GmbH, Europaplatz 3, 69115 Heidelberg,
Germany. If you have any concerns regarding our products, please
contact ProductSafety@springernature.com

Printed and bound by CPI Group (UK) Ltd, Croydon, CR0 4YY
29/04/2026
02099525-0010